I0213482

The Ladder of Prayer

What *A Course In Miracles* Teaches About Prayer,
Forgiveness and Healing

Also by brother hermit:

God Is: Ending Hell with *A Course In Miracles* (2017)
Available in softcover and hardcover edition from:

RiverSanctuaryPublishing.com

Amazon.com

The Ladder of Prayer

What *A Course In Miracles* Teaches About Prayer,
Forgiveness and Healing

brother hermit

River Sanctuary
PUBLISHING

The Ladder of Prayer

Copyright © 2019 by brother hermit

All rights reserved. No part of this book may be reproduced, stored in a retrieval system, or transmitted, in any form or by any means, electronic, mechanical, photocopying, recording, or otherwise, without the written prior permission of the author, except in the case of brief quotations embodied in critical articles and reviews.

All quotes from *A Course In Miracles*© are from the 3rd Edition, Combined Volume, EACIM-V, published in 2007. They are used with written permission from the copyright holder and publisher, The Foundation for Inner Peace, P.O. Box 598, Mill Valley, CA 94942-0598, www.acim.org and info@acim.org.

ISBN 978-1-935914-87-7

Printed in the United States of America

To order additional copies please visit:

www.riversanctuarypublishing.com

RIVER SANCTUARY PUBLISHING
P.O Box 1561
Felton, CA 95018
www.riversanctuarypublishing.com
Dedicated to the awakening of the New Earth

Dedicated to All Lovely and Holy Sisters.

With a respectful bow to my Holy Mother, Alicen (1934-2017)

Oh my God! What a beautiful Mind we share!

You are as certain of arriving home
as is the pathway of the sun laid down before it rises,
after it has set,
and in the half-lit hours in between.
Indeed, your pathway is more certain still.

~ A Course In Miracles

ACKNOWLEDGMENTS

I am grateful to the artist, Anne, who provided a forest wilderness sanctuary where I parked my bus and lived in solitude while I wrote this book, without the usual distractions. I was blessed to meet three bears in three weeks.

I am also grateful to my publisher, River Sanctuary Publishing. They are a blessing to me and a joy to work with.

My gratitude also to the persons of prayer I met at the following monasteries I am blessed to have lived at or visited since 1974:

New Camaldoli, Camaldolese Hermitage, Big Sur, California

New Clairvaux Abbey, Cistercian, Vina, California

St. Benedict's Abbey, Cistercian, Snowmass, Colorado

The Monastery of Christ in the Desert, Benedictine, near Abiquiu, New Mexico

Our Lady of Guadalupe Abbey, Benedictine, Pecos, New Mexico

Our Lady of the Redwoods Monastery, Cistercian, Whitethorn, California

Contents

PREFACE

*I*n *God Is* (2017), I discussed *A Course In Miracles* (ACIM or the course), how I found it, and why I embraced the teaching. I did not discuss a relationship with the course community because there is not much to discuss. Now, however, I wish to share more specifically about how I was influenced by various course teachers.

When I discovered and began reading ACIM in early 1992, I was impressed. The course seemed like the most advanced spiritual teaching I ever read. I came to it heavily conditioned by the Catholic Church and New Testament writings and did not know if it was true or not. The truth is I studied the course almost in complete isolation. To this day (June 2019) I never attended a course conference, course retreat or workshop, or even a course lecture. I never met nor communicated with any course teacher, well-known or not. This may seem strange, but I never even knew another course student! And yes, I am a hermit, so maybe that helps make sense of it. I never had any relationship with the course community, except for reading some course authors, and even that was minimal, as I now describe.

After a few weeks of studying the course I wondered what others might be saying about it. This was before I had Internet and I forget how I researched this. I read a Gerald Jampolsky book that introduced the course to me, but today I do not remember which book it was. I discovered two course authors, Tara Singh and Marianne Williamson. I do not remember reading a Tara Singh book, but I subscribed to his newsletter. I had many newsletters, all about the course. I no longer have these and I do not remember what Singh said about the course. I read Williamson's *A Return To Love*, and *A Woman's Worth*, yet I do not remember what she said about the course. Over the intervening 27 years those writings did not stay in my mind. The reason why I forgot them is because I read them but did not study them. Even with sustained and focused study of ACIM I forget frequently. I still get the impression I am reading something new, that I did not understand before, or remember, despite many readings. It could be age and cognitive decline or it could be simple resistance to the Truth. I went once to the Unity Church in Anchorage in 1992 and attended a course study group. I only went once and never returned, though I am not sure why. It was also in 1992, within a few months of starting to study ACIM, that life changed severely. I described the ordeal of my divorce in the previous book. At the time, I made no connection between those difficult days and ACIM, but now I am not so sure.

So that was it until 2013, when I began a three-year retreat from the world and immersive study of the course. I did not have money to buy books, but my brother, an avid reader, lived nearby. He owned a large book collection and I borrowed a Kenneth Wapnick book from him, *The Most Commonly Asked Questions about A Course In Miracles*, co-authored with Wapnick's wife, Gloria. That was the first Wapnick book I read, and I was disappointed with it. My main problem with it was that one of the questions they answered was a question important to me as well, and I did not like the answer. Needless-to-say, I was not interested in reading more Kenneth Wapnick based on that first impression. I did read one more borrowed Wapnick book, *Absence of Felicity*, his biography of Helen Schucman, the scribe of ACIM. This book was interesting because it revealed the history of the course. I learned some things about Wapnick that endeared him to me, things I related to, such as his attraction to a monastic life after reading Thomas Merton, and his love for music. He even made a retreat at Merton's Trappist monastery in Kentucky, and was baptized a Catholic, because he wanted to be a monk.

Other than those two Wapnick books, the only other course author I read was Gary Renard. I was impressed with Renard's books and studied his first three books. Some of his ideas were not the course as I understood it, but at that point, and still now, I intend to lay aside all judgment, and felt no need to judge Renard or his writing. As explained above, because of a lack of involvement with the course community, other than the few books I read, I was unaware of any controversy or division in the course community relating to Renard other than what he reported in his writings. I later learned that Renard's view of the course is close to Wapnick's, but I did not consider them identical, even though I had not read much of Wapnick yet. After finishing *God Is* I decided to study Wapnick's writing. Since then, I bought most of his books, including the books published after Wapnick's death in 2013, such as *A Symphony of Love* (2017), and *From the Lighthouse* (2015). These two books I highly recommend. The 40 pages of tributes to Kenneth Wapnick in *From the Lighthouse* are consistently loving and grateful regards towards this advanced teacher of God. This suggests that Kenneth Wapnick taught ACIM not so much with his classes, lectures, and books, but by demonstration. I am still reading through his large body of work, and so far it looks like my understanding is similar to Wapnick's and Renard's views.

I based *God Is* on an intensive and immersive study of the course itself, and the approach to this book is the same. Commentaries on the course, as is this book you are reading now, are useful to students but do not substitute for going directly to ACIM. Because I quote from the course frequently, the reader will read not only the commentary, but part of ACIM itself, and all of *The Song Of Prayer*. Some of the more spiritually radical parts of ACIM are like 193-proof everclear and therefore hard to consume straight. So even though here it is diluted with my commentary, it is still potent and the writer urges the reader to go slow.

I will share one more thing about the course before moving on to this book about prayer, forgiveness, and healing. As a baby-boomer, I share a common trait of boomers: aversion to authority. I rebelled against all authority, from Dad, to the church, to the Bible, to a boss, to the government, and uniforms like the police. I resisted any authority and my motto was: *You are not the boss of me.* I was like a wild animal that hated any kind of cage or leash. After studying the course for a while, however, I recognized it as a rational and spiritual authority I could accept and accept *easily*. As I see it, the content of ACIM is not of human origin. The teaching is superior to human authority and seems truer than anything else I read, including the Bible, Rumi, and J. Krishnamurti, all of whom I studied. Hence, I put faith in ACIM, and this faith is stronger than ever.

I intend to share understandings about ACIM is such a way as to be as brief, clear, and true as I can, with help from the Helper. I do not ask that you agree with me, nor believe any interpretation of ACIM. I do ask that you study the course quotes provided (the best part of this book) and see how *you* understand it, not how I understand it.

All quotes from *A Course In Miracles*© are from the 3rd Edition, Combined Volume, EACIM-V, published in 2007. The quotes are presented in two ways. Some quotes are presented in bold and indented. Other quotes are presented in italics within the commentary. References to quotes in *A Course In Miracles* are noted as follows:

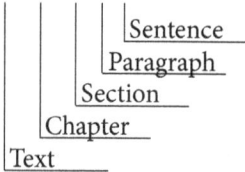

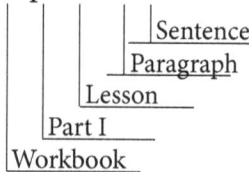

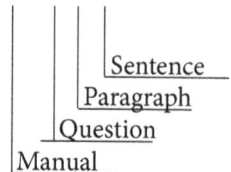

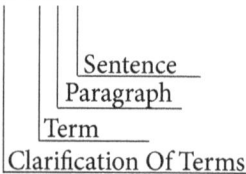

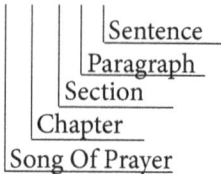

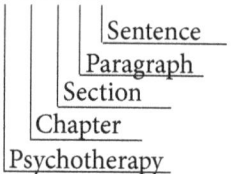

INTRODUCTION

*T*he *Song Of Prayer* is part of ACIM and offers its students a profound and advanced teaching about prayer, forgiveness, and healing. Students familiar with ACIM recognize major course themes such as true forgiveness, the Atonement, identity, relationships, the world and perception of form as illusionary, and the radical teachings about time. Forgiveness and healing are major course themes, but for most of us, including the writer, prayer does not jump out as a major theme. There is the course's version of the "Lord's Prayer," at the end of Chapter 16 of the *Text* (T-16.VII.12:1-7). There is not much more than that in the lengthy *Text*, only a few one or two liners, in terms of formal prayers, except for the end of the *Text*.

Here is the first of the final three paragraphs where Jesus shifts into prayer:

> I thank You, Father, for these holy ones who are my brothers as they are Your Sons. My faith in them is Yours. I am as sure that they will come to me as You are sure of what they are, and will forever be. They will accept the gift I offer them, because You gave it [to] me on their behalf. And as I would but do Your holy Will, so will they choose. And I give thanks for them. Salvation's song will echo through the world with every choice they make. For we are one in purpose, and the end of hell is near. (T-31.VIII.10:1-8)

The above prayer to the Father reminds me of the prayer Jesus prays at the Last Supper, in John's Gospel. It is a unitive prayer where Jesus thanks the Father for the unity of all: *For we are one in purpose.* The prayer also addresses God's Will: *And as I would but do Your holy Will, so will they choose.* In the last chapter of this book several prayers from the *Workbook* Part II pertaining to will are presented. The musical metaphor of song is used here and throughout *The Song Of Prayer*. In the prayer above: *Salvation's song will echo through the world.*

In the prayer below, the 2nd of the three final paragraphs of the *Text*, the song metaphor continues. Thanksgiving and trust in God's Will are repeated:

> **In joyous welcome is my hand outstretched to every brother who would join with me in reaching past temptation, and who looks with fixed determination toward the light that shines beyond in perfect constancy. Give me my own, for they belong to You. And can You fail in what is but Your Will? I give You thanks for what my brothers are. And as each one elects to join with me, the song of thanks from earth to Heaven grows from tiny scattered threads of melody to one inclusive chorus from a world redeemed from hell, and giving thanks to You. (T-31.VIII.11:1-5)**

The two uses of upper case *You* above refer to the Father. Many of the prayers Jesus gives in ACIM express thanks to God the Father: *I give You thanks for what my brothers are.* The previous two quotes mention hell: *...the end of hell is near* and *a world redeemed from hell.* The result of this liberation is gratefulness. The *song of thanks* grows as each of us chooses to join with Jesus.

The final words of the *Text* are a prayer to the Father describing the joyful ending of the journey to the Father: union. This union is described as a mutual indwelling. We dwell in Christ and Christ dwells in the Father: *For we have reached where all of us are one.*

> **And now we say "Amen." For Christ has come to dwell in the abode You set for Him before time was, in calm eternity. The journey closes, ending at the place where it began. No trace of it remains. Not one illusion is accorded faith, and not one spot of darkness still remains to hide the face of Christ from anyone. Thy Will is done, complete and perfectly, and all**

creation recognizes You, and knows You as the only Source it has. Clear in Your likeness does the light shine forth from everything that lives and moves in You. For we have reached where all of us are one, and we are home, where You would have us be. (T-31.VIII.12:1-8)

Thy Will be done is now *Thy Will is done,* completely and perfectly. After 669 pages of the *Text,* with only a few prayers and little teaching about prayer, the final three paragraphs are a prayer, a song of thanksgiving to the Father. The return to Heaven is complete: *all creation recognizes You, and knows You as the only Source it has.*

Although there are few prayers in the *Text,* there are many in the *Workbook.* In Part I of the *Workbook,* prayers start with Lesson 71. We are told to ask God specifically:

What would You have me do?

Where would You have me go?

What would You have me say, and to whom? (W-pI.71.9:3-5)

This prayer is about seeking God's will, as are many of the prayers in Part II of the *Workbook,* but specifically. Other parts of the course also speak about praying for specifics. In a workshop by Kenneth Wapnick called *The Nothingness of Something* © 2009 he suggests that Jesus gave us *The Song Of Prayer* about a year after the apparent completion of ACIM as a *correction.* Because students misunderstood the teaching about praying for specifics, clarification is given. Clarification is also given about healing and forgiveness.

For writing purposes, I use the electronic version of ACIM. For personal study and reading, I prefer the form of the book. I use the same copy of ACIM I bought in 1992, the 2nd Edition, Combined Volume. At that time the supplements to ACIM, *Psychotherapy,* and *The Song Of Prayer,* scribed in the same way and with the same source as

ACIM, were not included with the course as they are now. As a result, I did not read them for a long time. I find this delay ironic because I trained and worked as a psychotherapist without ever reading the pamphlet on psychotherapy!

ACIM is about 1250 pages of dense, concentrated, Shakespearian style writing that is almost overwhelming in its size, style, and content. There is so much there to study, for lifetimes, that what could the 22-page teaching, *The Song Of Prayer*, really add to the immense course? Quite a bit, surprisingly. Part of the brilliance of *The Song Of Prayer* is that it is so short, only about two percent of the entire course. The full ACIM is massive and might seem daunting. As a student becomes more and more familiar with the course, it becomes simpler and simpler because the same ideas are repeated over and over, using different words.

I do not remember when I first read *The Song Of Prayer*, but during and after one careful reading I was astonished at how much deep spiritual wisdom Jesus shares in 22 pages. I have a monastic background, and my primary monastic interest is contemplative prayer, different from the usual prayer of petition. This book is based mostly on *The Song Of Prayer* although relevant teachings and quotes from the *Text*, *Workbook*, and *Manual For Teachers*, *Clarification Of Terms*, and *Psychotherapy* are presented as well. All these writings are part of ACIM. Chapters 2, 3, and 4 of this book correspond to chapters 1, 2, and 3 of *The Song Of Prayer*.

Early in ACIM, Jesus teaches about prayer and the relationship between prayer, miracles and Love. In *The Song Of Prayer*, He focuses on the relationships between prayer and forgiveness, prayer and healing, and the various levels of prayer using the metaphor: the ladder of prayer. *The Song Of Prayer* also offers a short but sublime teaching about death, and that is presented in the fourth chapter of this book. To whet the reader's appetite for what is to come, here is a quote from *The Song Of Prayer*, in fact, the first sentence of this beautiful teaching:

Prayer is the greatest gift with which God blessed His Son at his creation. (S-in.1:1)

Wait.

What?

Prayer is the greatest gift God gave us?

Who knew?

How many course students consider prayer to be the greatest grace God gives? I did not know it myself until I studied *The Song Of Prayer*. The form of prayer that is God's greatest gift is not the usual understanding of prayer, and that is why this teaching is advanced. Why is prayer the greatest gift God gave us? Because in true prayer we commune with God, through the Holy Spirit, in stillness and silence, without words or thoughts.

This book assumes the reader is somewhat familiar with ACIM. Many of the important terms the course uses, such as forgiveness and Atonement do not have the same meanings as commonly understood. I explained this in the first book and I do not repeat that here, but the Teacher, Who is Jesus, does repeat Himself in *The Song Of Prayer*, and throughout ACIM. You do not need to be a course student to understand this book. If you are unfamiliar with the course, then some of the ideas will be challenging. An open mind is important. Anyone sincerely interested in mature, contemplative prayer, can benefit from this book.

Chapter One

PRAYER, LOVE, AND MIRACLES

A *Course In Miracles* first mentions prayer on the first page of the *Text* in the eleventh miracle principal. In three sentences it gives a definition of prayer, the purpose of prayer, and the relationship between prayer, miracles, and Divine Love. Earlier on the same page, in the third miracle principal, Jesus teaches about the relationship between Love and miracles. This third miracle principal prepares students for the eleventh principal, where prayer is first mentioned.

Here is the third miracle principal, also three sentences, followed by the eleventh:

> Miracles occur naturally as expressions of love. The real miracle is the love that inspires them. In this sense everything that comes from love is a miracle. (T-1.I.3:1-3)

> Prayer is the medium of miracles. It is a means of communication of the created with the Creator. Through prayer love is received, and through miracles love is expressed. (T-1.I.11:1-3)

In the third miracle principal Jesus teaches that miracles are natural expressions of Love, inspired by Love, and that Love makes miracles. Then in the eleventh miracle principal, He teaches that *prayer is the medium of miracles* because we receive Divine Love in prayer and then extend this Love through miracles. If we wish to join with Jesus and become miracle-minded miracle workers, healers, and teachers, then we learn how to pray truly and participate in the Love exchange.

1

Course students might experience confusion about praying to our Father because ACIM states in the *Manual For Teachers* that God does not understand words:

God does not understand words, for they were made by separated minds to keep them in the illusion of separation. (M-21.1:1)

We developed language and words because of separation from God. Although we could not achieve separation from God, God allows us to experience what separation is like in a dream detour. In the dream-time of pseudo-independence, we forgot about the non-symbolic, direct communication, or Holy Communion, that is our original way of communicating with God, Mind in Mind. Words and thoughts are used in the dream, not in Heaven. The development of prayer will lead to praying without words or thoughts.

So here is a challenge for course students: on the one hand, Jesus teaches that God does not understand words, because words are part of the dream of separation, illusionary, and symbols twice removed from reality (God *is* Reality). On the other hand, Jesus presents many prayers to the Father using words, throughout the course, but especially in Part II of the *Workbook*. Part II of the *Workbook* contains Lessons 221-365 and every one of these lessons contains a short prayer to the Father using words, except the final five lessons. The last five lessons still use words in prayer but now the prayer is addressed to the Holy Spirit instead of the Father. The words of these prayers are fairly minimal and designed to introduce a period of still, silent, wordless, thoughtless, and receptive prayer.

This kind of seeming inconsistency (using words to pray when God does not understand words) is best understood as level confusion. Jesus teaches from different levels. One is the absolute, non-dual level of God, Awareness, Truth, Knowledge, Divine Love, Heaven, Pure Joy, and Peace beyond understanding. This level is unspeakable and infinite. Finite words cannot describe the infinite. Even so, some mystics make *raids on the unspeakable* because *Except you share it, nothing can exist.* (T-28.V.1:10) Another level is the level I appear to be on here in the dualistic dream-world. These two levels, the absolute and the relative, are not compatible. Course students will benefit by learning how to hold in mind two ideas that might seem contradictory. From the viewpoint of Heaven, God does not understand words. From the human viewpoint, I use words to communicate, and to pray, until I learn a truer way. Jesus teaches the solution to this dilemma in ACIM. As we learn how to pray and how not to pray, the Holy Spirit prepares us to commune eternally with our Father in Heaven.

I will not presume to know the nature of God through words, intellect, or books, including ACIM. Only the experience of God leads to the Truth of God, and this experience is God's gift and He gives it when I am ready. The words, "God is Love," are as true as words can be, yet the experience of God's Love is beyond any words in any book, including the Bible, ACIM, or any other spiritual teaching. Divine Love is unspeakable. To be clear, God is Unconditional Divine Love, not love as human's use the word. Divine Love is to human love as the sun is to the moon. The sun is far more powerful and the source of the moonlight, yet it is painful to look at the sun for long. The moon is easy on the eyes.

Jesus calls the direct, non-symbolic communion between God and Creation *revelation*, and this is our original form of communing with God. Although revelation proceeds only from God to me, the love I receive in revelation can be shared. This love-sharing is the miracle. Jesus works with the Holy Spirit to bring about revelation because He understands *revelation-readiness*. I am ready for revelation when I can receive it without fear.

Revelations are indirectly inspired by me because I am close to the Holy Spirit, and alert to the revelation-readiness of my brothers. I can thus bring down to them more than they can draw down to themselves. The Holy Spirit mediates higher

> to lower communication, keeping the direct channel from
> God to you open for revelation. Revelation is not reciprocal.
> It proceeds from God to you, but not from you to God. When
> you return to your original form of communication with
> God by direct revelation, the need for miracles is over.
> (T-1.II.5:1-5)

Not only is the need for miracles over, but the necessity for words, thoughts, forgiveness, and healing is over as well. When do these needs disappear? When I return to the grace of true prayer, the original form of Holy Communion with God that never ends, which the course calls *direct revelation*.

Jesus goes back and forth between the non-dual and the dual in His teaching in order to minimize and eliminate fear. There are many forms of the truth expressing the same *content*. The *form* of the Atonement will vary according to how it is expressed, and to whom it is expressed. Yet the content of the Atonement does not change. An open mind, regarding the form in which Truth is expressed, is good.

> The value of the Atonement does not lie in the manner
> in which it is expressed. In fact, if it is used truly, it will
> inevitably be expressed in whatever way is most helpful to
> the receiver. This means that a miracle, to attain its full
> efficacy, must be expressed in a language that the recipient
> can understand without fear. This does not necessarily mean
> that this is the highest level of communication of which he is
> capable. It does mean, however, that it is the highest level of
> communication of which he is capable *now*. The whole aim
> of the miracle is to raise the level of communication, not to
> lower it by increasing fear. (T-2.IV.5:1-6)

Truth *will inevitably be expressed in whatever way is most helpful to the receiver.* Therefore the form of Truth varies, yet the content does not change. ACIM is understood by a student in whatever way is most helpful to her. So, not necessarily in the same formal way as another student.

Jesus teaches us to discern between form and content in the first chapter of the *Manual For Teachers*:

> There is a course for every teacher of God. The form of the course varies greatly. So do the particular teaching aids involved. But the content of the course never changes...It can be taught by actions or thoughts; in words or soundlessly; in any language or in no language; in any place or time or manner. It does not matter who the teacher was before he heard the Call. (M-1.3:1-4;6-7)

There are many different forms of teaching the truth, and many different teaching aids, yet the content does not change. The Truth can be taught *soundlessly*, without language. Still, I use words in the meantime, as I prepare to make a different choice.

I read in one of Kenneth Wapnick's books that Jesus uses *deceptive* language in ACIM. It might seem strange to say such a thing, but it makes sense if understood. The absolute truth might frighten us and so Jesus teaches the truth in such a way as to minimize fear. In the Gospels, Jesus taught that He had more to reveal, but the Apostles could not understand it, or accept it, yet. I find interesting the passages in ACIM where Jesus refers to His life on earth some 2,000 years ago. Here is one:

> As you read the teachings of the Apostles, remember that I told them myself that there was much they would understand later, because they were not wholly ready to follow me at the time. I do not want you to allow any fear to enter into the thought system toward which I am guiding you. (T-6.I.16:1-2)

Why were the Apostles not *wholly ready* to follow Jesus at that time? In a word: fear. Imagine how shocked and frightened the Apostles and followers of Jesus were at His crucifixion. Romans designed execution by crucifixion to be as painful, humiliating, and lingering as possible. Why make death as slow and excruciating as possible? To control people with fear. It was a successful form of terror. Now, with ACIM, Jesus does not want any fear blocking our understanding and practice.

In ACIM Jesus discusses the crucifixion and the implications are significant. This teaching about the cross and freedom from fear demonstrates that ACIM is not Christian, even though the teacher is Jesus.

The crucifixion is nothing more than an extreme example. (T-6.I.2:1)

The real meaning of the crucifixion lies in the *apparent* intensity of the assault of some of the Sons of God upon another. This, of course, is impossible, and must be fully understood *as* impossible. Otherwise, I cannot serve as a model for learning. (T-6.I.3:4-6)

The crucifixion of Jesus was designed to teach us that assault, no matter how extreme it seems, is not real. The crucifixion *represents release from fear to anyone who understands it.* (T-6.I.2:6)

The last thing Jesus wants to do is to cause fear because fear blocks the awareness of Love's Presence, and a goal of the course is to remove that block. For clarity, Love is not blocked, but the awareness of Love's presence is seemingly, and temporarily, blocked. Understanding what ACIM teaches will change and evolve as one climbs the ladder of prayer, and one needs to be able to relinquish a previous, less mature understanding, as one goes through the purification of immature-minded thinking. The Holy Spirit works with students in whatever way is most helpful to each student. This is an important approach in the genius of ACIM. It presents the highest teaching of non-duality, and at the same time offers a gradual approach to the Truth, as I acclimate to *freer air* at a base camp in duality.

I remember the beautiful toothless smile of my daughter. Tooth-less is gently harmless. She can't really bite anything, yet. If I gave a toothless baby a hunk of tough steak, it might taste good to the baby, but can she chew it? Not only can she not chew it, she is likely to choke on it and die. Before she can chew meat, she grows teeth, in fact two sets of teeth. I am a spiritual baby. Jesus does not want anyone chok-ing to death on His teaching. So, He starts out feeding us baby food (duality) and we will receive adult food (non-duality) when we are able to benefit from it. There are different levels of prayer (rungs on the ladder of prayer), and I use the highest level of prayer that I am capable of *now*, not the highest level possible.

What about when it seems like God does not answer prayer? The course explains what is happening when I seem to fail at prayer:

> Everyone who ever tried to use prayer to ask for something
> has experienced what appears to be failure. This is not
> only true in connection with specific things that might
> be harmful, but also in connection with requests that are
> strictly in line with this course. The latter in particular might
> be incorrectly interpreted as "proof" that the course does not
> mean what it says. You must remember, however, that the
> course states, and repeatedly, that its purpose is the escape
> from fear. (T-9.II.1:1-4)

Because Jesus does not want to increase fear, answers to prayer may not come in the form I seem to want. The quote above, from Chapter 9 in the *Text* continues, and explains why it seems as if prayer fails:

> Let us suppose, then, that what you ask of the Holy Spirit is
> what you really want, but you are still afraid of it. Should this
> be the case, your attainment of it would no longer *be* what
> you want. This is why certain specific forms of healing are
> not achieved, even when the state of healing is. An individual
> may ask for physical healing because he is fearful of bodily

harm. At the same time, if he were healed physically, the threat to his thought system might be considerably more fearful to him than its physical expression. In this case he is not really asking for release from fear, but for the removal of a symptom that he himself selected. This request is, therefore, not for healing at all. (T-9.II.2:1-7)

If the answer to a prayer results in fear, it defeats the purpose of prayer, which includes freedom from fear. I may not think that I fear an answer to prayer, yet I am unaware of unconscious fears. Prayer can ask amiss and that is a subject in the next chapter.

The Deconstruction of Self-Concept

It turns out that how one prays is related to one's sense of identity. Who am I? Both ego and Holy Spirit are in the split mind. I can pray from ego or from the part of mind where the Holy Spirit dwells. The more radical teachings of Jesus are presented in ACIM and many of these truths are challenging to accept. Here is an example: the course teaches that we share one Mind, and our true Identity is not billions of individual minds. It also refers to the "sons" of God in the plural, and "minds" in the plural. The course itself clearly explains this dichotomy:

Why is the illusion of many necessary? Only because reality is not understandable to the deluded. Only very few can hear God's Voice at all, and even they cannot communicate His messages directly through the Spirit which gave them. They need a medium through which communication becomes possible to those who do not realize that they are spirit. A body they can see. A voice they understand and listen to, without the fear that truth would encounter in them. Do not forget that truth can come only where it is welcomed without fear. So do God's teachers need a body, for their unity could not be recognized directly. (M-12.3:1-8)

Because I am deluded, I can't handle the Truth. The absolute Truth is frightening until I am ready, willing, and able to receive It, know It, and accept It. The Truth is frightening not because of the Truth Itself, but because It shines a holy Light onto the illusions I believe, especially about my identity as a unique, independent, individual. This extension of the Light causes the shadows of illusion and doubt to disappear. I fear losing that specialness. The perception here of billions of people, the *many*, is an illusion needed to minimize fear. This seems pretty clear to me:

> **It should especially be noted that God has only *one* Son. (T-2.VII.6:1)**

This is the non-dual truth as it is in Heaven, not earth.

In the last chapter of the *Text*, in Section V, titled *Self-Concept versus Self* is a teaching about identity, and how I am confused about Identity, and instead identify with a concept of self that I constructed. The Holy Spirit is tasked with the gentle and gradual deconstruction of the self-made self:

> **A concept of the self is meaningless, for no one here can see what it is for, and therefore cannot picture what it is. Yet is all learning that the world directs begun and ended with the single aim of teaching you this concept of yourself, that you will choose to follow this world's laws, and never seek to go beyond its roads nor realize the way you see yourself. Now must the Holy Spirit find a way to help you see this concept of the self must be undone, if any peace of mind is to be given you. (T-31.V.8:1-3)**

The Holy Spirit does this undoing in such a way as to minimize fear, because when Truth threatens false identity, I feel fear. The Holy Spirit is the Helper Who finds a way to help gently deconstruct the errone-ous self-concept I made, in such a way as to minimize and eliminate fear. I-me-mine is a man-made cognitive construction. Self is God-created and remains as God created it: perfect and one. Peace of mind depends on this identity-correction. It is a gradual process:

> For otherwise, you would be asked to make exchange of what you now believe for total loss of self, and greater terror would arise in you. (T-31.V.8:5)

...*total loss of self* does not sound fun to us. But what if my only hope for freedom is in escape from the prison of self? How does the Holy Spirit do this?

> Thus are the Holy Spirit's lesson plans arranged in easy steps, that though there be some lack of ease at times and some distress, there is no shattering of what was learned, but just a re-translation of what seems to be the evidence on its behalf. (T-31.V.9:1)

Jesus teaches us to examine the evidence for what seems to be the world. And examine the evidence for a separate self. The Holy Spirit *asks if just a little question might be raised.* The Holy Spirit teaches Truth without increasing fear:

> Your concept of the world depends upon this concept of the self. And both would go, if either one were ever raised to doubt. The Holy Spirit does not seek to throw you into panic. So He merely asks if just a little question might be raised. (T-31.V.11:3-6)

From a different section of the last chapter of the *Text*:

> Salvation does not seek to use a means as yet too alien to your thinking to be helpful, nor to make the kinds of change you could not recognize. (T-31.VII.1:2)

The Holy Spirit works gently so as not to increase fear, and this is why Jesus teaches on different levels. A first-grader will not understand calculus no matter how well the teacher understands it.

The Importance of the Holy Spirit

Who is in charge of the deconstruction of me? The Holy Spirit is in charge *at my request*. She helps not only in the undoing of an illusory self; She is also necessary in true prayer.

Because I lost awareness of union at the separation, God provides a way to maintain communication while I sleep. God does this through the Holy Spirit Who is in our mind, and She translates prayer to God. The Holy Spirit is in the unique position of both understanding the dream of duality (which God does *not* understand), and She understands the non-symbolic, direct, and non-dual communication of God. Thus the Holy Spirit bridges the gap between the illusion of duality and the truth of non-duality. I cannot do this myself, and God does not know of dualistic illusion because it is not real; it literally does not exist. *Nothing unreal exists.* But because we do believe it exists, God places the Holy Spirit in our mind, to help us in our self-imposed exile, as we seem to climb the ladder of prayer from earth to Heaven. Without Her help we do not climb at all. And without each other we cannot climb at all. The Holy Spirit strides both worlds, illusionary and true, both dual and non-dual. The Holy Spirit is also the one Who makes our relationships holy, if we ask Her.

I like to gather several course quotes about the same subject from a variety of chapters in the course. What follows are twelve quotes from various sections and chapters of ACIM, that repeat, in different words each time, the same Truth about the Holy Spirit.

The Holy Spirit is described as the remaining Communication Link between God and His separated Sons. In order to fulfill this special function the Holy Spirit has assumed a dual function. He knows because He is part of God; He perceives because He was sent to save humanity. (C-6.3:1-3)

The Holy Spirit's dual function: knowing with God and perceiving like us.

> The Holy Spirit mediates higher to lower communication, keeping the direct channel from God to you open for revelation. (T-1.II.5:3)

> God does not guide, because He can share only perfect knowledge. Guidance is evaluative, because it implies there is a right way and also a wrong way, one to be chosen and the other to be avoided. By choosing one you give up the other. The choice for the Holy Spirit is the choice for God. God is not in you in a literal sense; you are part of Him. When you chose to leave Him He gave you a Voice to speak for Him because He could no longer share His knowledge with you without hindrance. Direct communication was broken because you had made another voice. (T-5.II.5:1-7)

What is the other voice I made? The voice of the autonomous ego, which is wrong-minded and hoarse from screaming about separation, sin, condemnation, guilt, fear, and death.

> The Holy Spirit is your Guide in choosing. He is in the part of your mind that always speaks for the right choice, because He speaks for God. He is your remaining communication with God, which you can interrupt but cannot destroy. The Holy Spirit is the way in which God's Will is done on earth as it is in Heaven. (T-5.II.8:1-4)

Prayer and the Holy Spirit work together to facilitate communication with God. Jesus teaches that I can interrupt this communication but not destroy it. Four more times She is described as the Communication Link.

> Remember that the Holy Spirit is the Communication Link between God the Father and His separated Sons. (T-6.I.19:1)

Being the Communication Link between God and His separated Sons, the Holy Spirit interprets everything you have made in the light of what He is. (T-8.VII.2:2)

God's remaining Communication Link with all His children joins them together, and them to Him. To be aware of this is to heal them because it is the awareness that no one is separate, and so no one is sick. (T-10.III.2:6-7)

The Holy Spirit is described as the remaining *communication with God*, and the *Communication Link* five times. She is what remains from what we once had, revelation without end. The second sentence above summarizes the fourth chapter on healing and also the Holy Spirits healing role in ending separation through joining. Healers heal through the awareness that no one is separate because sickness requires separation. The Holy Spirit is what joins us to Her and each other. Who does the Holy Spirit join together? All God's children.

The Communication Link that God Himself placed within you, joining your mind with His, cannot be broken. (T-13.XI.8:1)

God can communicate only to the Holy Spirit in your mind, because only He shares the knowledge of what you are with God. And only the Holy Spirit can answer God for you, for only He knows what God is. Everything else that you have placed within your mind cannot exist, for what is not in communication with the Mind of God has never been. Communication with God is life. Nothing without it is at all. (T-14.IV.10:3-7)

All this is safe within you, where the Holy Spirit shines. He shines not in division, but in the meeting place where God, united with His Son, speaks to His Son through Him.

> Communication between what cannot be divided cannot
> cease. The holy meeting place of the unseparated Father and
> His Son lies in the Holy Spirit and in you. (T-14.VIII.2:10-13)

> For the Holy Spirit, too, is a communication medium,
> receiving from the Father and offering His messages unto the
> Son. (T-19.IV.B.i.17:3)

> The Holy Spirit abides in the part of your mind that is part of
> the Christ Mind. He represents your Self and your Creator,
> Who are One. He speaks for God and also for you, being
> joined with Both. (C-6.4:1-3)

Jesus is consistent in His teaching about the Holy Spirit's role in connecting us to God. Here again is a radical teaching of non-duality: the Holy Spirit represents Self and Creator, *Who are One.*

In ACIM Jesus declares that He is the manifestation of the Holy Spirit:

> I am the manifestation of the Holy Spirit, and when you see
> me it will be because you have invited Him. (T-12.VII.6:1)

And this, where Jesus teaches about Christ:

> And He sees for you, as your witness to the real world. He is
> the Holy Spirit's manifestation, looking always on the real
> world, and calling forth its witnesses and drawing them to
> you. (T-13.V.9:4-5)

And in the *Clarification Of Terms* the nature of the Holy Spirit is described:

> Jesus is the manifestation of the Holy Spirit, Whom he called
> down upon the earth after he ascended into Heaven, or
> became completely identified with the Christ, the Son of God
> as He created Him. (C-6.1:1)

The above quote is interesting in terms of Christian theology. He translates *ascended into Heaven* into *became completely identified with the Christ*. When the Apostles could not accept Jesus telling them that He was leaving, that He was willingly going to the crucifixion, Jesus explained why He was doing this: if He did not go, He could not send the Holy Spirit to help them remember, to understand everything He taught, and finally, to follow Him.

> **I myself said, "If I go I will send you another Comforter and he will abide with you." (T-5.I.4:4)**

The passage above is another quote where Jesus refers to His life on earth. The Comforter is the Holy Spirit, Who is also called *Guide, Healer, Helper, Friend, Universal Inspiration*, and *The Voice for God*.

Jesus identified with the Holy Spirit and became the manifestation of the Holy Spirit. Now He wants all of us to become the manifestation of the Holy Spirit. As a single body (even used correctly to communicate the truth), He is limited. The above quote continues:

> **The Holy Spirit, being a creation of the one Creator, creating with Him and in His likeness or spirit, is eternal and has never changed. He was "called down upon the earth" in the sense that it was now possible to accept Him and to hear His Voice. His is the Voice for God, and has therefore taken form. This form is not His reality, which God alone knows along with Christ, His real Son, Who is part of Him. (C-6.1:2-5)**

Jesus is providing clarification about the Holy Spirit.

"Called down to the earth" is in quotes because He is offering a correction to the Christian doctrine. The Holy Spirit was not called down to earth when Jesus became fully identified with the Christ. God had already assigned the Holy Spirit to be in our mind at the instant we attempted separation. In the chapter on healing, Jesus teaches us to discern between receiving and accepting. A healing is always received when it is given, but it could be a while before a patient can accept the healing. The same is true about the Holy Spirit. God already gave Her to everyone at the instant the dream of separation started. We already received the Holy Spirit but may not yet accept this gift from God. Jesus was the first human to accept the Holy Spirit already in His mind. Thus He was the first to complete His part in the Atonement. Jesus is the prototype to demonstrate that we all can accept the Holy Spirit because He did. We are to follow Him. So what happened is that instead of calling the Holy Spirit down to the earth, we can now accept the Holy Spirit Whom God already gave: *He was "called down upon the earth" in the sense that it was now possible to accept Him and to hear His Voice.*

> **The Holy Spirit is in you in a very literal sense. His is the Voice that calls you back to where you were before and will be again. It is possible even in this world to hear only that Voice and no other. It takes effort and great willingness to learn. It is the final lesson that I learned, and God's Sons are as equal as learners as they are as Sons. (T-5.II.3:7-11)**

Jesus was the first the hear the Holy Spirit's Voice and he teaches that learning to hear only the Holy Spirit's Voice was *the final lesson* He learned. We are to follow Him and learn the same thing. Apparently, this final lesson is not easy and requires *effort and great willingness to learn.*

As a side note, the reason why Jesus calls the Holy Spirit the Voice *for* God, instead of the Voice *of* God is because God does not have a voice, just like God does not have a body. To speak of the voice of God is to anthropomorphize God. The Holy Spirit walks in two worlds, with one foot in the dream and one foot in Heaven, and She translates our human thoughts and wishes into the direct communication God understands, and this communication is unceasing. Jesus is not sloppy with the words He uses as we often are.

Another example of anthropomorphizing God is to give Him consciousness. I used to confuse the words consciousness and awareness and considered them to be symbols for the same phenomena, but Jesus teaches that they are not. The phrase, *the consciousness of God*, sounds holy, but you will not find that term in ACIM. Jesus explains why not:

> **Consciousness, the level of perception, was the first split introduced into the mind after the separation, making the mind a perceiver rather than a creator. Consciousness is correctly identified as the domain of the ego.** (T-3.IV.2:1-2)

To think or speak of the consciousness of God is the same as thinking or saying the ego of God. I know that in using terms like "consciousness of God" or "God's consciousness" the user of those terms does not intend to mean "God's ego." ACIM clearly makes this distinction that is useful here, yet not in Heaven. Skillful use of language does not confuse the consciousness of God with the Awareness of God. Ego perceives. God does not perceive. God Knows. God is Aware. God Is. Ising. I sing I Am That. I AM.

Is the Holy Spirit part of the illusion or eternal? She is both. One formal role is temporary and not Her *Reality*, but Her Identity, *which God alone knows*, is eternal as God. The Holy Spirit is eternal and has never changed. The Holy Spirit's *form* as the Voice for God however, is temporary and happened at the instant of separation. That role is not needed in Heaven. This distinction is clear, is it not? The Holy Spirit's importance to us as we journey back to Heaven is stressed again in the final five lessons of the *Workbook*, and the *Epilogue*.

When we accept the Holy Spirit we are following Jesus and can become the manifestation of the Holy Spirit as He did: *You are His manifestation in this world. Your brother calls to you to be His Voice along with him.* (C-6.1:5) Perhaps this is a question of logistics. Repeatedly, Jesus teaches that His course is practical. Regarding logistics, I did the math. Let's say Jesus returns to the earth as a body, coming in glory in the clouds with an army of angels, as many Christian's believe, the so-called Second Coming, after great tribulation. So now He rules His Kingdom on earth for a thousand years of peace. (Even though He already said that His Kingdom is not of this world.) Let's also say that all seven billion people on earth get to meet Him in person and Jesus wants this too. He plans to spend five minutes with each human person. These meetings go on 24/7 because Jesus does not need to sleep or eat. If Jesus spends five minutes with each person, it will take 60,000 years for everyone to meet Him, if my math is correct. Separation into billions of fragments is not practical. What is the solution? The Holy Spirit Who is literally in our mind gives everyone instant access to Jesus and the Whole Child of God.

I noticed that Kenneth Wapnick in his teaching would often say "Jesus or the Holy Spirit" because the words are only symbols and we could use any other symbol-word that works. I apply that truth in my own practice. I am fine saying Jesus or the Holy Spirit.

*   *   *

The importance and necessity for prayer is explained in ACIM on the first page of the *Text*. Miracle workers share love received in prayer. *Revelation* is the original way of communing with God and we are learning how to return to that. The truth, and answers to prayer, can only come when they are welcomed without fear. How I identify is a factor in how I pray. Because I identify with an erroneous concept of self, the Holy Spirit helps to undo and forget this wrong-minded thought system. The Holy Spirit is vital to correcting identity-confusion and She acts as the *remaining Communication Link* between God and His separated children. God is not aware of the dream, including the use of words to communicate. God's communication is non-symbolic and direct and the Holy Spirit bridges this gap between non-duality and duality.

Next, Jesus teaches about the different forms of prayer, from the egoic to the true song of prayer, using the metaphor *the ladder of prayer*.

Chapter Two

THE LADDER OF PRAYER

Introduction

The Song Of Prayer begins by presenting the true and holy form of prayer as it is in Heaven, even above the highest rung of the ladder of prayer. The ladder of prayer is part of duality and not needed in Heaven. Jesus teaches in a non-linear fashion. Generally, we are not used to this, but we may as well get used to it. In the first of three introductory paragraphs in *The Song Of Prayer*, Jesus starts off with the end:

> Prayer is the greatest gift with which God blessed His Son at his creation. It was then what it is to become; the single voice Creator and creation share; the song the Son sings to the Father, Who returns the thanks it offers Him unto the Son. Endless the harmony, and endless, too, the joyous concord of the Love They give forever to Each Other. And in this, creation is extended. God gives thanks to His extension in His Son. His Son gives thanks for his creation, in the song of his creating in his Father's Name. The Love They share is what all prayer will be throughout eternity, when time is done. For such it was before time seemed to be. (S-in.1:1-8)

This paragraph is so jam-packed with concentrated teaching, so pregnant with potent meaning, that it needs unpacking.

Because music is a favorite art for me in this world, I am happy that of all the metaphors Jesus might use to describe the prayer of Heaven, He uses music, the song. And He continues using this musical metaphor throughout *The Song Of Prayer*. One of the signs that this first paragraph is describing the holiest level of prayer is that the words referring to God's Son, including pronouns, are all uppercase and singular. In studying the course, students benefit by careful attention to detail such as if a word or pronoun is upper case or lower case, singular or plural. It helps to go slowly.

As already discussed, Jesus teaches that prayer is the greatest gift God gave us at our creation. Next we learn that this perfect form of prayer, that we seem to have forgotten because of the fall, we all are returning to: *It was then what it is to become.* Then He describes this prayer as a song of gratefulness and thanksgiving that God's Child (Creation) sings to the Father, and the Father sings to His Child, as a single voice. This teaching is a beautiful expression of non-duality. It might seem that it is expressing duality because there seems to be two, Father and Child, and non-duality means "not two," or "not dual." But it is non-dual because Father and Child share *one* voice. And this grateful song of the highest order never ends. It is not in time, nor limited by time. It is eternal. And it is not only this song of thanks We share, but Divine Love: *the joyous concord of the Love They give forever to Each Other.* Prayer at this mature stage is shared Love and this sharing never ends.

This sharing in one Love and one song with one voice is Creation, the extension of God. Therefore, when God gives thanks for His Child, He is giving thanks to His Extension, which is part of Him. And His Child gives thanks to Her Creator for Her creation. Because God created Her, He gave Her Existence, Being, Awareness, Love, Pure Joy, Peace, and Eternal Life. This is the fullness of life we experience again as we re-awaken to the Truth. When time is over, and we enter Eternal Life, true prayer remains *the Love They share,* forever. It is forever because time is temporary and the last day is coming. There is no time in Heaven, only the Holy Instant.

This first introductory paragraph of *The Song Of Prayer* introduces the highest form of prayer, literally the state of Heaven, before even mentioning the ladder of prayer and the lower forms of prayer. The word highest implies duality and the various levels of prayer from lowest to highest. But in non-dual Heaven there are no distinctions or different levels. In duality prayer can be false or true. Heaven does not have this dichotomy. This is part of the challenge of using a dualistic language to describe non-duality.

The Song Of Prayer uses the "ladder of prayer" as a metaphor for different levels of prayer, from the lowest to the highest, from earth to Heaven. In describing the various levels of prayer, Jesus continues His non-linear approach. There is not a nice and neat description of each rung on the ladder. In the genius of the Holy Spirit, prayer will take whatever form I most need.

To you who are in time a little while, prayer takes the form that best will suit your need. You have but one. (S-in.2:1-2)

This quote is a good example of how Jesus speaks of both levels, the non-dual and the dual, in a few words. He does this often. On the level of duality, we are the ones *in time a little while*. Yet in terms of non-duality we share only *one* need. Teaching that we share one need implies that we are the same.

In this dualist world there are different forms of prayer, different rungs on the ladder of prayer. In Heaven, there is only one form of prayer, the highest, or actually beyond the highest, because the word highest implies there are lower forms. Ideas of highest and lowest are concepts of duality that disappear in Heaven. If one reads the above quote without understanding the different levels it can seem confusing or even contradictory. On the one hand, prayer will take whatever form I seem to need. On the other hand, I have only one need. There are different expressions of the one need, in duality.

What is the one need we share? It is the need to recognize our wholeness: holy oneness with our Creator and Its Creation: Union. We are whole when everyone is included, without exception. Our growth in prayer depends on this realization. When this unity is realized, the result is gratitude and thanksgiving to God for ending the nightmare of separation. How do we come to this recognition? *Prayer now must be the means.* Remember, prayer is the greatest grace God gave us.

> What God created one must recognize its oneness, and rejoice that what illusions seemed to separate is one forever in the Mind of God. Prayer now must be the means by which God's Son leaves separate goals and separate interests by, and turns in holy gladness to the truth of union in his Father and himself. (S-in.2:3-4)

This might challenge some course students who consider true forgiveness to be the means, but patience please until Jesus explains that most important relationship between prayer and forgiveness, discussed in the next chapter. What is prayer the means for? It is the means by which we leave separation. We relinquish the ego's goals and interests and instead re-turn *in holy gladness to the truth of union.*

The next quote repeats some ideas already covered. Students of the course know that there is a lot of necessary repetition in the course because the teaching is so radical and different from what we already learned, especially what we learned about spirituality. It is easy to repeat ideas when you have 1,250 pages to do so. But even in *The Song Of Prayer* there is much repetition.

> Lay down your dreams, you holy Son of God, and rising up as God created you, dispense with idols and remember Him. Prayer will sustain you now, and bless you as you lift your heart to Him in rising song that reaches higher and then higher still, until both high and low have disappeared. Faith in your goal will grow and hold you up as you ascend the shining stairway to the lawns of Heaven and the gate of peace. For this is prayer, and here salvation is. This is the way. It is God's gift to you. (S-in.3:1-6)

Jesus teaches that prayer will sustain us and bless us. Prayer is again described as a song with different levels: *rising song that reaches higher and higher*. And again He presents both levels of duality and non-duality. Duality is the *higher and higher* until we reach non-duality, where *both high and low have disappeared*. He teaches that prayer is *salvation* and *the way*. Jesus demonstrates flexibility in switching metaphors…from the shining stairway to Heaven to the ladder of prayer. We are still in the *Introduction* and He has not mentioned the ladder of prayer yet. The above quote ends the *Introduction* to *The Song Of Prayer*'s first chapter: *Prayer*.

It really is impressive how much, and how deep, a teaching is presented in less than one page, three short paragraphs, that is only the *Introduction*. *The Song Of Prayer* is concentrated and pregnant with spiritual Truth, to the extent that Truth can be expressed with words. Actually, the whole course is that way. It points us in the direction to go until we get there. The meanings grow as we grow. I like how the three paragraph introduction ends:

> *For this is prayer, and here salvation is.*
> *This is the way. It is God's gift to you.*

True Prayer

Next, *The Song Of Prayer* starts to teach about the different levels of prayer and how at the lowest levels, it is not truly prayer, but the ego asking to get. The first line in the next quote repeats the definition and purpose of true prayer:

> **Prayer is a way offered by the Holy Spirit to reach God. It is not merely a question or an entreaty. It cannot succeed until you realize that it asks for nothing. How else could it serve its purpose? It is impossible to pray for idols and hope to reach God. True prayer must avoid the pitfall of asking to entreat. Ask, rather, to receive what is already given; to accept what is already there. (S-1.I.1:1-7)**

The above quote introduces the lower forms of prayer, both asking questions of God and asking for things that Jesus calls *idols*. Earlier in ACIM, He teaches that idols are anything anyone wants- person, place or thing, that one perceives as outside of oneself. Jesus is teaching us to discern the difference between false prayer and true prayer: *true prayer must avoid the pitfall of asking to entreat*, and: *it is impossible to pray for idols and hope to reach God*. Jesus asks us to ask about anything, *what is it for?* Remember what prayer is for: to connect with God, experience Holy Communion, and share Love with our Source and Cause, not to obtain idols and illusions of form that appear outside of me and are temporary.

ACIM teaches that God already gave His Child everything simply by creating Her to share God's own Being. So instead of praying for material things, we pray that we might recognize and accept what God already gifted, what is already and always true, now. The Atonement already happened. We are trying to catch up with it. The teachings about time are perhaps the most radical teachings in the course:

> This world was over long ago. The thoughts that made it are no longer in the mind that thought of them and loved them for a little while. (T-28.I.1:6-7)

> All the effects of guilt are here no more. For guilt is over. (T-28.I.2:1-2)

> Time is a trick, a sleight of hand, a vast illusion in which figures come and go as if by magic. Yet there is a plan behind appearances that does not change. The script is written. When experience will come to end your doubting has been set. For we but see the journey from the point at which it ended, looking back on it, imagining we make it once again; reviewing mentally what has gone by. (W-pI.158.4:1-5)

Early *Workbook* lessons 7, 8, and 9 are titled: (7) *I see only the past.* (8) *My mind is preoccupied with past thoughts.* (9) *I see nothing as it is now.*

The non-dual teaching above from the *Introduction* that we only have one need is repeated:

> You have been told to ask the Holy Spirit for the answer to any specific problem, and that you will receive a specific answer if such is your need. You have also been told that there is only one problem and one answer. In prayer this is not contradictory. (S-1.I.2:1-3)

Again, Jesus presents both levels in one quote and He even anticipates that we might interpret it as contradictory: *In prayer this is not contradictory.* This quote also refers back to His previous teaching in ACIM: *You have been told.* One answer to one problem: non-duality.

The Holy Spirit knows that on the level of this world, we appear to have needs. The next quote explains how this works out, how the Holy Spirit provides for our needs, even though these needs are illusions. This is also another quote that presents both levels. The truth is, I am not at the highest, or even higher rungs on the ladder, and the Holy Spirit understands that I cannot really grasp answers at the higher levels, so the answer to prayer, if from God, will suit the needs as I see them, but this is not the true answer to true prayer.

Continuing the musical metaphor of song, Jesus discerns between the echo of God's answer and the real sound of prayer, a song of thanksgiving and Love, as He taught in the first paragraph.

> There are decisions to make here, and they must be made whether they be illusions or not. You cannot be asked to accept answers which are beyond the level of need that you can recognize. Therefore, it is not the form of the question that matters, nor how it is asked. The form of the answer, if given by God, will suit your need as you see it. This is merely an echo of the reply of His Voice. The real sound is always a song of thanksgiving and of Love. (S-1.I.2:4-9)

Therefore, the echo is a secondary effect of the true song and dependent on it. Without the true song, there will be no echo. We are not asked *to accept answers which are beyond the level of need that you can recognize.* The Holy Spirit works with each of us in the way that we can best benefit and that means not in the same formal way.

The next paragraph continues the musical metaphor, adding to echo the terms overtones and harmonics. These are side effects of true prayer, but it is a mistake to pray for them.

> **You cannot, then, ask for the echo. It is the song that is the gift. Along with it come the overtones, the harmonics, the echoes, but these are secondary. In true prayer you hear only the song. All the rest is merely added. You have sought first the Kingdom of Heaven, and all else has indeed been given you. (S-1.I.3:1-6)**

The use of the word *indeed* above suggests a reference back to the famous Gospel quote by Jesus about seeking first, and eventually *only*, the Kingdom. Instead of praying for what we think we need, we seek first for the Kingdom (the *only* true need we have) and surrender all personal and little needs to God, trusting that whatever needs we seem to have in the dream, the Holy Spirit will provide for. I love the great line from the U2 song, *Beautiful Day*: *"What you don't have, you don't need it now."*

The next paragraph states that if we ask for specific things or people, we are engaging in false prayer, much like false forgiveness:

> **The secret of true prayer is to forget the things you think you need. To ask for the specific is much the same as to look on sin and then forgive it. Also in the same way, in prayer you overlook your specific needs as you see them, and let them go into God's Hands. There they become your gifts to Him, for they tell Him that you would have no gods before Him; no love but His. What could His answer be but your**

remembrance of Him? Can this be traded for a bit of trifling advice about a problem of an instant's duration? God answers only for eternity. But still all little answers are contained in this. (S-1.I.4:1-8)

Again, Jesus teaches both levels side by side. Praying for specifics is asking God *for a bit of trifling advice about a problem of an instant's duration* (duality). All the problems we seem to experience here are temporary…here today, gone tomorrow. The non-dual level: *God answers only for eternity.* The earthly dualistic level: *But still all little answers are contained in this.* These little answers are the echoes, the overtones, the harmonics, that are effects of the Eternal Answer, the everlasting song of thanksgiving, the One Love we share.

The ladder of prayer represents more of a continuum than precise levels. It helps students to understand this in advance. Next, Jesus describes true prayer higher up the ladder:

Prayer is a stepping aside; a letting go, a quiet time of listening and loving. It should not be confused with supplication of any kind, because it is a way of remembering your holiness. Why should holiness entreat, being fully entitled to everything Love has to offer? And it is to Love you go in prayer. Prayer is an offering; a giving up of yourself to be at one with Love. There is nothing to ask because there is nothing left to want. That nothingness becomes the altar of God. It disappears in Him. (S-1.I.5:1-8)

Here Jesus teaches a higher form of prayer that is more contemplative: *a stepping aside, a letting go, a quiet time of listening and loving, an offering, a giving up of yourself to be at one with Love.* We see again the relationship between prayer and Love already described in the eleventh miracle principal. How often do we think of prayer as a way to be at one with Love? How often do we think of prayer as listening rather than supplication? In order to listen, I am quiet. If I interrupt, I am not listening. Listening in prayer is challenged by the ego's accusing, noisy, and loud screaming of its grudges, grievances, judgment, and condemnation. The ego does not want us to connect with God in prayer. The ego always speaks first and loudest. The Holy Spirit does not have to holler. I like Bob Dylan's lyric from *Like a Rolling Stone*: *Now you don't talk so loud, Now you don't seem so proud.*

I heard a story about the saint, Mother Teresa of Calcutta. A journalist asked her if she prayed. She replied, "Yes." Then the reporter asked her what she says to God. Her reply: "I don't say anything; I listen." Next he asked her, "What does God say?" Mother Teresa answered, "He doesn't say anything; He listens." I was surprised when I found out that Kenneth Wapnick and Bill Thetford knew Mother Teresa personally. I understand she tried to recruit Bill to come to India and work with her. Wapnick speaks highly of her.

In *God Is* I described a wonderful experience of deep peace. It only lasted a few minutes, but at the heart of it was an utter contentment; I wanted nothing: *there is nothing to ask because there is nothing left to want.* This kind of prayer is high up the ladder.

> **This is not a level of prayer that everyone can attain as yet. Those who have not reached it still need your help in prayer because their asking is not yet based upon acceptance. Help in prayer does not mean that another mediates between you and God. But it does mean that another stands beside you and helps to raise you up to Him. One who has realized the goodness of God prays without fear. And one who prays without fear cannot but reach Him. He can therefore also reach His Son, wherever he may be and whatever form he may seem to take. (S-1.I.6:1-7)**

The phrase above, *their asking is not yet based upon acceptance*, refers back to the earlier verse: *Ask, rather, to receive what is already given; to accept what is already there.* Our prayer is to thank the Father for what is already given and always true. Jesus also teaches here that to help someone in prayer is not mediation between her and God. Instead I join with her, praying with her as an equal. To pray without fear is a higher level of prayer because fear of God is the final obstacle to peace. It does not matter what form anyone takes because there is no difference between us.

ACIM teaches that the Holy Spirit is literally in our mind. Praying to Christ in anyone is an interesting idea.

> **Praying to Christ in anyone is true prayer because it is a gift of thanks to His Father. To ask that Christ be but Himself is not an entreaty. It is a song of thanksgiving for what you are. Herein lies the power of prayer. It asks nothing and receives everything. This prayer can be shared because it receives for everyone. To pray with one who knows that this is true is to be answered. Perhaps the specific form of resolution for a specific problem will occur to either of you; it does not matter which. Perhaps it will reach both, if you are genuinely attuned to one another. It will come because you have realized that Christ is in both of you. That is its only truth. (S-1.I.7:1-11)**

Praying to Christ in a sister is recognizing her true Identity as Christ, and when we do that we recognize our shared Identity as Christ, in Christ. A sister is the mirror in which I know Self. And for this recognition of each other as one Christ, we give thanks to our Father for the truth of What-We-Are, still as He created us. ACIM teaches a type of prayer that is receptive and does not ask for anything. Even when a specific answer is given, that is secondary, an echo, that comes because we recognize each other as sharing the same Identity as Christ, the one Child of God, the extension of God, the dwelling place of God. Again Jesus presents both levels. Specific problems and answers are part of the dualistic dream. Non-duality: *That is its only truth.* Joined together we are one Christ.

The Ladder of Prayer

Since prayer has no beginning or end, prayer is eternal. In this way it is different from forgiveness, which is a temporary key used to unlock the junkie jail cell.

> Prayer has no beginning and no end. It is a part of life. But it does change in form, and grow with learning until it reaches its formless state, and fuses into total communication with God. In its asking form it need not, and often does not, make appeal to God, or even involve belief in Him. At these levels prayer is merely wanting, out of a sense of scarcity and lack. (S-1.II.1:1-5)

Forgiveness is part of the dream and not needed in Heaven, but prayer continues in Heaven without end, just as eternal life is without end. The two levels again appear in one sentence. Prayer evolves as we climb the ladder from this dualistic world *until it reaches its formless state, and fuses into total communication with God.* If prayer is petitioning God for idols of this world, then I am low on the ladder and this prayer is coming from the needy ego's projected reality of scarcity and lack.

One of the main themes of ACIM is understanding our true Identity as the one Child of the Father, *still as God created us.* How I identify myself is a factor in how I pray.

> These forms of prayer, or asking-out-of-need, always involve feelings of weakness and inadequacy, and could never be made by a Son of God who knows Who he is. No one, then, who is sure of his Identity could pray in these forms. Yet it is also true that no one who is uncertain of his Identity can avoid praying in this way. And prayer is as continual as life. Everyone prays without ceasing. Ask and you have received, for you have established what it is you want. (S-1.II.2:1-6)

On the lower rungs of the ladder we pray out of perceived neediness, which demonstrates that we do not know What-We-Are. In the passage above the word Identity is upper case, indicating our true Identity as Christ. When we do not realize our true Identity we cannot help but to pray from the lower rungs.

In the same paragraph above, Jesus teaches: *Everyone prays without ceasing*; prayer is continual. This brings to mind the quote from St. Paul, encouraging us to *pray without ceasing*. Orthodox monks, hermits, and pilgrims try to fulfill this by praying the Jesus Prayer, constantly, counting each prayer on beads. But here He is saying that we automatically pray without ceasing; prayer is built into us by God, because we never stop Holy Communion with God, even if one is unaware of this Communion. That prayer is unceasing is confirmed in *Workbook* Lesson 49:

> **The part of your mind in which truth abides is in constant communication with God, whether you are aware of it or not. (W-pI.49.1:2)**

Even though prayer is continual, we pray according to where we are in the spiritual journey. We cannot pray truly as the Child of God until we know that we are the Creation of God. Before that, we pray in lesser ways. This can't be avoided. The last phrase, *for you have established what it is you want*, indicates that desire is prayer; whatever I desire I am praying for.

The next paragraph describes an intermediate rung on the ladder of prayer. This is a shift above the lowest rungs, *a higher form of asking-out-of-need*, but is still immature.

> **It is also possible to reach a higher form of asking-out-of-need, for in this world prayer is reparative, and so it must entail levels of learning. Here, the asking may be addressed to God in honest belief, though not yet with understanding. A vague and usually unstable sense of identification has**

generally been reached, but tends to be blurred by a deep-rooted sense of sin. It is possible at this level to continue to ask for things of this world in various forms, and it is also possible to ask for gifts such as honesty or goodness, and particularly for forgiveness for the many sources of guilt that inevitably underlie any prayer of need. Without guilt there is no scarcity. The sinless have no needs. (S-1.II.3:1-6)

One's sense of identity is starting to shift but is still vague and *unstable*. The dualistic world *must entail levels of learning*. At this level one might still ask for things of this world, but also ask for *gifts such as honesty or goodness, and particularly for forgiveness*. Behind neediness, and prayers of petition, is guilt, and when guilt is removed through true forgiveness, I am no longer needy. Notice how Jesus describes identity at this stage: a vague sense of identity is *blurred by a deep-rooted sense of sin*: guilt. Then He switches to the non-dual: *Without guilt there is no scarcity. The sinless have no needs.* Without sin and guilt means without the ego, or identifying as a separate individual, and I am not yet that high on the ladder, and this is reflected in how I pray.

In the next paragraph, Jesus describes another example of this intermediate level of prayer, known as *praying for one's enemies*. He calls this form of prayer a *curious contradiction*.

At this level also comes that curious contradiction in terms known as "praying for one's enemies." The contradiction lies not in the actual words, but rather in the way in which they are usually interpreted. While you believe you have enemies, you have limited prayer to the laws of this world, and have also limited your ability to receive and to accept to the same narrow margins. And yet, if you have enemies you have need of prayer, and great need, too. What does the phrase really mean? Pray for yourself, that you may not seek to imprison

Christ and thereby lose the recognition of your own Identity.
Be traitor to no one, or you will be treacherous to yourself.
(S-1.II.4:1-7)

If I am praying for enemies, it represents a lower rung on the ladder
because I am still under the delusion that I have enemies. If I believe
in enemies prayer is *limited to the laws of the world*. This goes back
to my sense of identity. If I identify someone as an enemy, I fail to
understand that this "enemy" is actually a part of Our Self, the Christ
Child of God. The so-called enemy is perceived as an enemy because
I have projected secret guilt onto her. Being in this conflicted state
limits prayer, but at the same time, if we still believe in enemies, we
have need of prayer, and great need too. If I have an enemy I am a traitor to myself because the enemy is part of Christ, as am I. To have an
enemy is to imprison Christ because I will not perceive this enemy as
Christ, even though that is the alleged enemy's true Identity. Imagine
praying to Christ in someone you dislike or consider an enemy.

Instead of praying for enemies, I pray for myself, that I be healed
of the guilt I projected. The more guilt I project is the more guilt I
keep. I pray that the distorted and guilty perception of others that I
hold be healed, so that I see them *as they are*, not as the enemies I
made by projecting guilt onto them. Soon Jesus teaches that I only
ever pray for myself.

> An enemy is the symbol of an imprisoned Christ. And who
> could He be except yourself? The prayer for enemies thus
> becomes a prayer for your own freedom. Now it is no longer
> a contradiction in terms. It has become a statement of the
> unity of Christ and a recognition of His sinlessness. And now
> it has become holy, for it acknowledges the Son of God as he
> was created. (S-1.II.5:1-6)

My perception of anyone is corrected by seeing her through the forgiving eyes of Christ, or the vision of Christ. This Christ-view is not

visual. I see with mind, not eyeballs. I look past the visible body and understand that this is a holy sister, no different from me, and with the exact same and single need I have. I understand that she is sinless, still as God created her. If I pray in this way, instead of praying for enemies, prayer becomes holy and a statement of the unity of Christ. In recognizing any sister's innocence, I recognize my own. In freeing her from projection, I am freed from projecting. This higher rung of prayer is for My Self, that I might see everyone not as enemy, but as Self, holy and still as God created It.

I am both enemy/ego and Christ as long as I suffer the identity-confusion ACIM refers to as *split mind*.

> **Let it never be forgotten that prayer at any level is always for yourself. If you unite with anyone in prayer, you make him part of you. The enemy is you, as is the Christ. Before it can become holy, then, prayer becomes a choice. You do not choose for another. You can but choose for yourself. Pray truly for your enemies, for herein lies your own salvation. Forgive them for your sins, and you will be forgiven indeed. (S-1.II.6:1-8)**

The last sentence of the above quote repeats Jesus' radical turnaround teaching about forgiveness. Unless the reader is already familiar with this course teaching, this sentence is hard to understand: *Forgive them for your sins.* This is an already well-established course teaching:

> **Yet think on this, and learn the cause of faithlessness: You think you hold against your brother what he has done to you. But what you really blame him for is what you did to him. It is not his past but yours you hold against him. (T-17.VII.8:1-3)**

By projecting guilt onto a sister, I make her an enemy, and I will fail to realize that she is actually Christ, as am I. I do not forgive a sister her "sins." I forgive myself for projecting my guilt onto her. I withdraw this projection, and she is no longer seen as sinful. This is how I now receive forgiveness myself: by removing the projection of guilt I am freed from the guilt of attacking her. We are forgiven together, or not at all.

The next paragraph is a completely level one non-dual statement, except for the first sentence that describes the spiritual journey through duality as we climb the ladder of prayer to non-duality.

> **Prayer is a ladder reaching up to Heaven. At the top there is a transformation much like your own, for prayer is part of you. The things of earth are left behind, all unremembered. There is no asking, for there is no lack. Identity in Christ is fully recognized as set forever, beyond all change and incorruptible. The light no longer flickers, and will never go out. Now, without needs of any kind, and clad forever in the pure sinlessness that is the gift of God to you, His Son, prayer can again become what it was meant to be. For now it rises as a song of thanks to your Creator, sung without words, or thoughts, or vain desires, unneedful now of anything at all. So it extends, as it was meant to do. And for this giving God Himself gives thanks. (S-1.II.7:1-10)**

At the top of the ladder there is a transformation of prayer as there is a transformation of identity. Remember the first sentence from *The Song Of Prayer*, where Jesus teaches that God gave His greatest gift to us, prayer, at our creation? This ability to commune with God is hard-wired into us and therefore a transformation of identity is also a transformation of prayer, a return to the true prayer that was before the separation, and still is now, a song of thanksgiving that the Father and Daughter sing with one voice to each other, forever, without words or thoughts. When we reach the top of the ladder, *the things of earth are left behind, all unremembered.*

Those nine verses above are another amazing example of how Jesus can say so much in so few words. It is concise and rich in meaning. The phrase, the *light no longer flickers*, implies that until we reach the top of the ladder of prayer, the light will probably flicker, and so we might expect that, and not let ourselves be discouraged when we experience both darkness and light as we ascend. In the teaching about death in Chapter Four, Jesus teaches that here we can only *reach the Christ in hidden forms and clearly seen at most in lovely flashes*. When our perception changes, we are blessed to view Christ without blinders.

The next quote describes how the ladder of prayer and the lower forms of prayer are an illusion because, as the Atonement teaches, the separation never happened.

> **God is the goal of every prayer, giving it timelessness instead of end. Nor has it a beginning, because the goal has never changed. Prayer in its earlier forms is an illusion, because there is no need for a ladder to reach what one has never left. Yet prayer is part of forgiveness as long as forgiveness, itself an illusion, remains unattained. Prayer is tied up with learning until the goal of learning has been reached. And then all things will be transformed together, and returned unblemished into the Mind of God. Being beyond learning, this state cannot be described. The stages necessary to its attainment, however, need to be understood, if peace is to be restored to God's Son, who lives now with the illusion of death and the fear of God. (S-1.II.8:1-8)**

Because we believe that the separation did happen, the ladder of prayer is provided to us as one means of escaping the prison.

The above quote also teaches that the non-duality of Heaven *cannot be described*; that state is *beyond learning*. Yet Jesus does sneak in a preview: *And then all things will be transformed together, and returned unblemished into the Mind of God.* But before we get there we learn the means necessary to dissolve the illusions we still believe. To be clear, the ladder of prayer is part of duality and temporary, but true prayer is non-dual and non-temporal: it is everlasting because Holy

Communion with the Father never ends. We seem to climb the ladder of prayer through duality to arrive at non-duality, in the dream. In this quote Jesus teaches that prayer is part of forgiveness: *Yet prayer is part of forgiveness as long as forgiveness, itself an illusion, remains unattained.* Prayer is temporarily *tied up with learning*, until we are ready for what is beyond learning. When forgiveness is complete learning is complete, and prayer can jettison the booster rocket that helped her rise above gravity. Then prayer returns to its true orbit, the song of prayer in Inner Space.

Praying for Others

The next quote starts a discussion about praying for others, and how this prayer fits into the ladder of prayer, and it repeats the earlier teaching in *The Song Of Prayer*, about praying for one's enemies.

We said that prayer is always for yourself, and this is so. Why, then, should you pray for others at all? And if you should, how should you do it? Praying for others, if rightly understood, becomes a means for lifting your projections of guilt from your brother, and enabling you to recognize it is not he who is hurting you. The poisonous thought that he is your enemy, your evil counterpart, your nemesis, must be relinquished before you can be saved from guilt. For this the means is prayer, of rising power and with ascending goals, until it reaches even up to God. (S-1.III.1:1-6)

Prayer for another, *if rightly understood*, is prayer for myself, that I might remove the projection of guilt, that I placed onto a sister, consciously perceived as enemy or not. This form of prayer fuses into a form of forgiveness. Whenever I project guilt onto any sister, I make her an enemy and imprison the Christ in her, by not recognizing our equality: in truth we are the same, not different, and not sinful. The judgmental and accusing thought that a sister is an enemy, that she hurt someone by her sin, is a *poisonous thought*, a toxic ego thought, that I must relinquish if I am to be free of guilt myself, and *for this the means is prayer.*

The last sentence from the quote above is one of those double level statements. Duality: *rising power and ascending goals*; non-duality: *until it reaches even up to God.* The word until shows the temporary nature of the climb.

In the next paragraph Jesus reviews the ego type prayer at the bottom of the ladder, where, because of guilt, we make God into a *vengeful god.*

> **The earlier forms of prayer, at the bottom of the ladder, will not be free from envy and malice. They call for vengeance, not for love. Nor do they come from one who understands that they are calls for death, made out of fear by those who cherish guilt. They call upon a vengeful god, and it is he who seems to answer them. Hell cannot be asked for another, and then escaped by him who asks for it. Only those who are in hell can ask for hell. Those who have been forgiven, and who accepted their forgiveness, could never make a prayer like that. (S-1.III.2:1-7)**

Imagine prayers to defeat an enemy or prayers for revenge. The lowest rungs of the ladder actually represent the "prayers" of the ego. We start where we are. There are two parts to forgiveness. First it is given to us. This already happened. Yet we will experience a delay in the benefits of forgiveness and prayer until we accept what God has already given: *Those who have been forgiven, and who accepted their forgiveness...*If I accept the forgiveness God already gave, I will not pray falsely for revenge. Before I accept forgiveness I experience hell because I asked for hell. If I pray for vengeance, I am asking for hell, and that is what I get.

The first step in learning to pray truly is to realize I am praying in the wrong way. The above quote is a review that sets up the next paragraph:

At these levels, then, the learning goal must be to recognize that prayer will bring an answer only in the form in which the prayer was made. This is enough. From here it will be an easy step to the next levels. The next ascent begins with this:

What I have asked for for my brother is not what I would have. Thus have I made of him my enemy. (S-1.III.3:1-6)

I learn that prayer will be answered only in the form that the prayer takes. I learn not to pray for anything that I do not want for myself. Whatever I pray for someone else is prayer for myself. The last two sentences in the quote above are italicized for emphasis and demonstrate an important shift in how we pray above the lowest rungs. This is the shift to seeing everyone as the same underneath the masks we wear as we play our parts in the drama. This is the first of three such ideas that describe the development of prayer in terms of *relationship*.

This first major shift is difficult because freeing enemies appears dangerous, like letting a killer out of prison, and so this shift may be long delayed.

It is apparent that this step cannot be reached by anyone who sees no value or advantage to himself in setting others free. This may be long delayed, because it may seem to be dangerous instead of merciful. To the guilty there seems indeed to be a real advantage in having enemies, and this imagined gain must go, if enemies are to be set free. (S-1.III.3:7-9)

True prayer is shared and we will not likely share prayer with anyone considered an enemy. The guilty need enemies on whom they project their guilt. Without guilt, there is no need for enemies.

This teaching about prayer continues about the dynamics between prayer and relationship. The guilt that I learn to see as illusion I hide in two places. One is the unconscious mind. Then this hidden guilt is projected onto another so that I can maintain the bogus belief that I am not guilty, but she is. Freedom from guilt can only happen *in the recognition that the guilt has gone.* This is the meaning of the Atonement. Real guilt was never there in the first place, only the belief in guilt.

Jesus teaches that *sin is lack of love* (T-1.IV.3:1) and *Every mistake must be a call for love.* (T-19.III.4:7) The claim of sin is forgiven, not actual sin. This healing is in the mind, where the *belief* in sin and separation is squatting for a season. It is better to think of sin as a mistake that is a call for love. Any mistake we feel guilty about is not real and has no real effects because the mistake only seemed to happen in the dream. Even so, the Holy Spirit knows how to take our mistakes, our calls for love, and use them as classrooms where we learn our lessons to be free. Yet we fear setting enemies free; keeping an enemy isolated in jail helps us feel safe. Therefore, I am not free of guilt if I have hidden it in the unconscious mind or in a sister, and since she is a terrorist, she should be locked up, so I feel safe. Thus, to be free of guilt I free whomever I mistakenly laid guilt upon. If guilt is swept under the rug, it is not gone.

> Guilt must be given up, and not concealed. Nor can this be done without some pain, and a glimpse of the merciful nature of this step may for some time be followed by a deep retreat into fear. For fear's defenses are fearful in themselves, and when they are recognized they bring their fear with them. Yet what advantage has an illusion of escape ever brought a prisoner? His real escape from guilt can lie only in the recognition that the guilt has gone. And how can this be recognized as long as he hides it in another, and does not see it as his own? Fear of escape makes it difficult to welcome freedom, and to make a jailer of an enemy seems to be safety. How, then, can he be released without an insane fear for yourself? You have made of him your salvation and your escape from guilt. Your investment in this escape is heavy, and your fear of letting it go is strong. (S-1.III.4:1-10)

Our own ignorant plan for salvation is to avoid guilt by concealing it in another. This is a psychological defense mechanism named projection and it is maintained with denial. I resist the truth that what really bothers me about another person is within me. I deny the problem is my own by seeing it in a sister. Because the investment in this ego plan for hiding guilt via projection is so heavy, we are reluctant to let it go. The ego intends to maintain its kingdom of separation with fear.

Next, Jesus reminds us about the course teaching about responsibility. I made someone an enemy and I can reverse this and make her a friend, and instead understand that she is the same as I am, the one Daughter of God, the Christ. Then the so-called enemy becomes a blessing. Her freedom is my freedom.

> **Stand still an instant, now, and think what you have done. Do not forget that it is you who did it, and who can therefore let it go. Hold out your hand. This enemy has come to bless you. Take his blessing, and feel how your heart is lifted and your fear released. Do not hold on to it, nor onto him. He is a Son of God, along with you. He is no jailer, but a messenger of Christ. Be this to him, that you may see him thus. (S-1.III.5:1-9)**

Responsibility has two parts. I did this, and, I undo this. I learn to see anyone as a messenger of Christ as I be this messenger myself.

In the next quote Jesus teaches that praying *for things, for status, for human love, for "gifts" of any kind* is a mistake because seeking these external idols is an attempt to hide from guilt and use these things as inappropriate substitutes for God, and thus locking us up in the jail of duality. He also states that it *is not easy* for us to realize this.

> **It is not easy to realize that prayers for things, for status, for human love, for external "gifts" of any kind, are always made to set up jailers and to hide from guilt. These things are used for goals that substitute for God, and therefore distort**

the purpose of prayer. The desire for them is the prayer. One
need not ask explicitly. The goal of God is lost in the quest
for lesser goals of any kind, and prayer becomes requests for
enemies. The power of prayer can be quite clearly recognized
even in this. No one who wants an enemy will fail to find one.
But just as surely will he lose the only true goal that is given
him. Think of the cost, and understand it well. All other
goals are at the cost of God. (S-1.III.6:1-10)

We pray not only in formal prayer, but also through desire. Desire
is prayer of the heart. Do I desire God or lesser goals? Praying for
these lesser goals does not have to be explicit: *The desire for them is
the prayer.* What we want is what we are praying for *without ceasing.*
The cost we pay for desiring anything but God is heavy. Desiring only
God is the advanced state of a heart that is purified of lesser goals.
What we desire is what we *will* for.

Praying with Others

Remember that the first level of growth in prayer comes with
the realization that I am praying or desiring something for someone
else that I do not want for myself, and thus I make an enemy of her.
I learn to stop praying in the wrong way. The second level of growth
is described next, and is the prerequisite for praying with others, or
joining in prayer. Again, this idea is expressed in terms of relationship: *We go together, you and I.*

Until the second level at least begins, one cannot share in
prayer. For until that point, each one must ask for different
things. But once the need to hold the other as an enemy
has been questioned, and the reason for doing so has been
recognized if only for an instant, it becomes possible to join
in prayer. Enemies do not share a goal. It is in this their

enmity is kept. Their separate wishes are their arsenals; their fortresses in hate. The key to rising further still in prayer lies in this simple thought; this change of mind:

We go together, you and I. (S-1.IV.1:1-8)

True prayer is shared. We do not share prayer with enemies because we want different things and these desires are prayer. To get to this higher level of shared prayer, this simple change of mind, I question *the need to hold the other as an enemy.* And even if I recognize why I did this for *only an instant,* that is enough to *join in prayer.* Why do I make enemies? Because of the belief in guilt.

This joining in prayer means we begin the quicker ascent, but still have many lessons to learn. Yet at the beginning of this shared prayer, we can still pray in an immature way.

> Now it is possible to help in prayer, and so reach up yourself. This step begins the quicker ascent, but there are still many lessons to learn. The way is open, and hope is justified. Yet it is likely at first that what is asked for even by those who join in prayer is not the goal that prayer should truly seek. Even together you may ask for things, and thus set up but an illusion of a goal you share. You may ask together for specifics, and not realize that you are asking for effects without the cause. And this you cannot have. For no one can receive effects alone, asking a cause from which they do not come to offer them to him. (S-1.IV.2:1-8)

Even if we join in prayer, we can still can fall into the error of asking for things, specifics, and lesser goals that are *shared desires.* In this case we are praying for effects, the echoes and harmonics of true prayer and Jesus teaches us to give up this mistake and pray only the true prayer of thanksgiving and not pray for the side-effects that we may desire. And if we desire them, we are praying for them. The last sentence of the quote above teaches that because God is not the cause of the specific dream effects we might desire, we should not pray for them.

The simple way to avoid the mistake of asking for specific things is instead to pray, *Thy Will be done*, and in this prayer all specifics are answered.

> **Even the joining, then, is not enough, if those who pray together do not ask, before all else, what is the Will of God. From this Cause only can the answer come in which are all specifics satisfied; all separate wishes unified in one. Prayer for specifics always asks to have the past repeated in some way. What was enjoyed before, or seemed to be; what was another's and he seemed to love, –all these are but illusions from the past. The aim of prayer is to release the present from its chains of past illusions; to let it be a freely chosen remedy from every choice that stood for a mistake. What prayer can offer now so far exceeds all that you asked before that it is pitiful to be content with less. (S-1.IV.3:1-6)**

The Will of God is the Cause we should pray for. When we pray for specifics, we are praying for something known about and desired from the past. What we enjoyed before we want to repeat, or what we suffered in the past we pray to avoid. This emphasis on the past goes against one purpose of prayer which is to free the present moment from being chained to the past. True prayer offers a portal to the present free of the past and future. Praying for specifics is asking God to make the dream future like the dream past, which He does not do. When we make this mistake, we try to keep the past, which makes us miserable.

If we unite in praying for God's Will, we find relief from our previous mistakes in prayer, when we asked for shared desires. So instead of asking God to give us things, idols, or any inappropriate substitute for the Father, we pray: *Thy Will be done*. What if God's Will is for far more than we can imagine? We exchange all wanting for dream specifics for the one desire for God's Will, which will include all the echoes and harmonics, in ways better than we can direct, plan, or even imagine. It is *pitiful* if we settle for less than the best by asking for personal desires rather than the mighty Will of God.

If we pray for, or desire, specifics, even together, we are restricting prayer to limited and time-bound things, idols that quickly crumble into dust.

> **You have chosen a newborn chance each time you pray. And would you stifle and imprison it in ancient prisons, when the chance has come to free yourself from all of them at once? Do not restrict your asking. Prayer can bring the peace of God. What time-bound thing can give you more than this, in just the little space that lasts until it crumbles into dust? (S-1.IV.4:1-5)**

Every time we pray we receive a *newborn chance* to free ourselves from *ancient prisons*. The *peace of God* that this kind of prayer brings, is worth far more than any and all *time-bound things*. Where are ancient prisons? In the past.

The Ladder Ends

As we ascend to the higher rungs of the ladder, we receive true humility. ACIM often uses the word "true" before many words, such as forgiveness, Love, and healing, because how Jesus uses these words is different from the common and traditional. True as an adjective implies there is a different version of the word. He teaches that humility brings peace because I let go of control and surrender all will to control to the true Authority. Humility also permits a ceasing of judgment because humility knows that I cannot judge even if I want to, because *I do not know.* At this point we are nearing the top of the ladder.

> **Prayer is a way to true humility. And here again it rises slowly up, and grows in strength and love and holiness. Let it but leave the ground where it begins to rise to God, and true**

> humility will come at last to grace the mind that thought it
> was alone and stood against the world. Humility brings peace
> because it does not claim that you must rule the universe, nor
> judge all things as you would have them be. All little gods
> it gladly lays aside, not in resentment, but in honesty and
> recognition that they do not serve. (S-1.V.1:1-5)

The mind thought it was alone and opposed to the world. The truth
is the mind is not alone but joined with all minds into one Mind and
we have no need to oppose the world. If the world is not real, why
would we oppose it? We only oppose it because we think it is real.

True humility will not compromise with what is not humble, just
as light cannot compromise with darkness. In the *Text*, Jesus tells us
that ACIM is easy if we do not compromise, but difficult if we do:

> This course is easy just because it makes no compromise. Yet
> it seems difficult to those who still believe that compromise is
> possible. (T-23.III.4:1-2)

When we are truly humble we no longer need the illusion of enemies,
nor idols, nor defense: *little gods*. At this purified stage, we have *no
goal but God*.

> Illusions and humility have goals so far apart they cannot
> coexist, nor share a dwelling place where they can meet.
> Where one has come the other disappears. The truly humble
> have no goal but God because they need no idols, and defense
> no longer serves a purpose. Enemies are useless now, because
> humility does not oppose. It does not hide in shame because
> it is content with what it is, knowing creation is the Will of
> God. Its selflessness is Self, and this it sees in every meeting,
> where it gladly joins with every Son of God, whose purity it
> recognizes that it shares with him. (S-1.V.2:1-6)

Jesus teaches in the paragraph above a poetic truth about humility: *Its selflessness is Self.*

Because *humility does not oppose,* we can meet every Child of God as our Self instead of as the little selfish imp. A humble sister does not need enemies and accepts everyone as no different from her. Once humility is established, the ladder of prayer rises above the world, bodies, and all false idols. Now we see everyone as innocent and sinless. Now we are near the top of the ladder: *High has the ladder risen.* Humility teaches us to understand our *glory* as God's Creation. To believe in sin is arrogance.

> Now prayer is lifted from the world of things, of bodies, and of gods of every kind, and you can rest in holiness at last. Humility has come to teach you how to understand your glory as God's Son, and recognize the arrogance of sin. A dream has veiled the face of Christ from you. Now can you look upon His sinlessness. High has the ladder risen. You have come almost to Heaven. There is little more to learn before the journey is complete. Now can you say to everyone who comes to join in prayer with you:
>
> *I cannot go without you, for you are a part of me.*
>
> And so he is in truth. Now can you pray only for what you truly share with him. For you have understood he never left, and you, who seemed alone, are one with him. (S-1.V.3:1-12)

Near the end of the paragraph above, Jesus teaches the third thought, again italicized for emphasis, that describes relationship at the top of the ladder: *I cannot go without you, for you are a part of me.* This is the recognition of the oneness that we share as the one Child of God. We are part of each other. Together we have climbed the ladder from a stage where *there are still many lessons to learn* to the stage where *there is little more to learn before the journey is complete.* Remember, learning can only take us so far. Then we move beyond learning, which cannot be described with the finite symbology of language.

Now, finally, we have ascended to the top of the ladder. Now I am joined with a beautiful and pure sister and we stand together, as holy equals, *at the place appointed for the time when you should come.* This is the place where time ends forever, and this place, the *gate of Heaven, has waited long for you.* Together we exchange the dualistic world of time, where everything is temporary, for the glory of non-dual-eternal-life-everlasting.

> **The ladder ends with this, for learning is no longer needed. Now you stand before the gate of Heaven, and your brother stands beside you there. The lawns are deep and still, for here the place appointed for the time when you should come has waited long for you. Here will time end forever. At this gate eternity itself will join with you. Prayer has become what it was meant to be, for you have recognized the Christ in you. (S-1.V.4:1-6)**

Now prayer returns to its proper place, as described in the Introduction to *The Song Of Prayer*: the song of thanksgiving that the Daughter and the Father sing to each other with one Voice. Now, *learning is no longer needed.* When I realize my true Identity as Christ I re-join the song of prayer in Heaven, the true prayer which is what prayer was meant to be and will be for all eternity. The quote above ends the first of the three chapters, only eight pages, in *The Song Of Prayer*.

In summary, Jesus teaches three broad levels of growth in prayer, or ascending the ladder from earth to Heaven, that He presents in three thoughts or changes in the mind. The quality of prayer is described in terms of relationship. Notice how one leads naturally to the next. Here they are again:

1. *What I have asked for for my brother is not what I would have. Thus have I made of him my enemy.* (S-1.III.3:5-6)

2. *We go together, you and I.* (S-1.IV.1:8)

3. *I cannot go without you, for you are a part of me.*
   (S-1.V.3:9)

It starts with realizing that I am praying in the wrong way, a way that actually does harm, making someone an enemy, and demonstrating the lie of separation. Next, I realize that we join to climb together. This not a solo climb. Finally, we learn of our unity, sameness, and oneness. I cannot climb the ladder of prayer without you because: Sisters-Я-Us. That's the ticket! To be clear, minds are joined, not bodies.

In describing where one is on the ladder of prayer in terms of relationship, Jesus is preparing us for the next chapter, where He teaches about the crucial relationship between prayer and forgiveness.

Chapter Three

PRAYER AND FORGIVENESS

*P*robably, the most emphasized teaching in ACIM is about true
forgiveness. Now, in *The Song Of Prayer*, Jesus teaches illumi-
nating and clarifying ideas about forgiveness.

I explained in *God Is* the use of sexist, male-biased language in
the course and why I chose to follow the course's example. I am not a
body and therefore I am not female or male, and neither is God, Jesus,
or the Holy Spirit. Yet I hear this as a body where gender seems a fact.
I also said it didn't matter if I used male-biased language or female-
biased language because such dualistic, sexist, and exclusive language,
either way, emphasizes body-identity. Gender, that separates us into
opposite sexes, is a temporary illusion of duality. It is not so in Heaven.

In the *Introduction* to the chapter on forgiveness in *The Song
Of Prayer*, Jesus uses the word *sister* for the only time in the entire
course. In this book I am following that example by using feminine
language when I can. I also use inclusive terms that are genderless
like everyone, anyone, one, we, our, us, or you when I can. It really
does not matter. Yet the male bias is still there in the course quotes,
which I do not change. Despite the male-biased language in ACIM,
it came through a female scribe and one of the major and repeated
teachings in the course is about a radical, unconditional equality
and oneness of everyone regardless of all the ways we have divided
ourselves into separate and often opposing factions including gender,
sexual orientation, race, religion, nationality, language, socioeconomic
status, age, and so on. Clearly our Teacher is not exclusive or sexist.
If anyone is upset about language that *seems* exclusive it is because
one is identified with a category of humans and excluded others. If I

am exclusive, I will interpret what I read as exclusive. On the surface your skin is a different color than mine. But underneath our blood is the same red color. We are not different. We are the same one Child of God, disguised as different. It is always Halloween here.

As I study the course, I find it important to go slow and study carefully. A quick reading of the quote below from the *Text* might seem inconsistent with *The Song Of Prayer*, but not with a careful reading.

> **But the only meaningful prayer is for forgiveness, because those who have been forgiven have everything. Once forgiveness has been accepted, prayer in the usual sense becomes utterly meaningless. The prayer for forgiveness is nothing more than a request that you may be able to recognize what you already have.** (T-3.V.6:3-5)

The quote above might be interpreted as once I accept forgiveness, then prayer is *utterly meaningless*. But a careful read will show that a particular form of prayer becomes meaningless: *prayer in the usual sense*. The usual sense means the usual and common prayer of supplication, or asking for, or desiring, a nicer duplex in duality. Jesus teaches that since the Father already gave us everything, there is nothing left to ask for: *those who have been forgiven have everything.* These usual forms of prayer are lower on the ladder of prayer. The last line in the above quote confirms the earlier teaching in *The Song Of Prayer*, that we pray to recognize and accept what is already true: *The prayer for forgiveness is nothing more than a request that you may be able to recognize what you already have.* What we already have: God's Love and blessing of forgiveness, both unconditional. We all have already received these blessings from God the Father but we all have not yet accepted these holy gifts. In the Gospels, Jesus thanked His Father for hearing and answering His prayer *before* there was any external evidence that God had heard and answered. Jesus knew that it was already true. Most of us believe what our senses show us over the truth that cannot be seen with the eyes nor heard with the ears.

Introduction

In the *Introduction* to the second chapter in *The Song Of Prayer*, *Forgiveness*, Jesus teaches that the integration of prayer and forgiveness keeps our *feet secure* and our purpose *steadfast* and *unchangeable*. This is also the only time He uses the word sister in the entire course and He uses it twice:

> **Forgiveness offers wings to prayer, to make its rising easy and its progress swift. Without its strong support it would be vain to try to rise above prayer's bottom step, or even to attempt to climb at all. Forgiveness is prayer's ally; sister in the plan for your salvation. Both must come to hold you up and keep your feet secure; your purpose steadfast and unchangeable. Behold the greatest help that God ordained to be with you until you reach to Him. Illusion's end will come with this. Unlike the timeless nature of its sister, prayer, forgiveness has an end. For it becomes unneeded when the rising up is done. Yet now it has a purpose beyond which you cannot go, Nor have you need to go. Accomplish this and you have been redeemed. Accomplish this and you have been transformed. Accomplish this and you will save the world. (S-2.in.1:1-12)**

Without forgiveness, we will not climb above the lowest rung of the ladder of prayer and we might as well not even try to make the climb: *it would be vain to try to rise above prayer's bottom step.*

Prayer is called the *sister* of forgiveness, and forgiveness offers *wings to prayer*. Climbing the ladder of prayer is easier with wings. Actually, we can't climb the ladder to Heaven at all without forgiveness. We need both prayer and forgiveness to climb the ladder: *both must come to hold you up.* In the first sentence of *The Song Of Prayer*, Jesus describes prayer as the greatest gift God gave us. Above He uses the term *the greatest help*. This seems to be about both forgiveness and prayer working together, or their integration. The last three lines of the quote above say that once we truly forgive, the ladder of prayer is no longer needed and we are *redeemed, transformed,* and we will save the world by no longer judging the world as full of sin.

To save the world might seem inconsistent with the previous *Workbook* Lesson 132:

> There is no world! This is the central thought the course attempts to teach. Not everyone is ready to accept it, and each one must go as far as he can let himself be led along the road to truth. He will return and go still farther, or perhaps step back a while and then return again. (W-p1.132.6:2-5)

> But healing is the gift of those who are prepared to learn there is no world, and can accept the lesson now. Their readiness will bring the lesson to them in some form which they can understand and recognize. Some see it suddenly on point of death, and rise to teach it. Others find it in experience that is not of this world, which shows them that the world does not exist because what they behold must be the truth, and yet it clearly contradicts the world. (W-p1.132.7:1-4)

> And some will find it in this course, and in the exercises that we do today. (W-p1.132.8.1)

Now if the central thought the course tries to teach is the radical teaching that *There is no world*, why does Jesus teach here and in many other places about *saving the world*? It behooves us to remember that the course uses words in original ways that are not the same as the meanings we learned in school. We save the world by forgiving the world and releasing it from guilty projection. This is clarified late in ACIM:

> The world is saved from what you thought it was. And what it is, is wholly uncondemned and wholly pure. (C-2.9:4-5)

The world is perceived by way of projection, and built on the foundation of separation, sin, guilt, and fear. Save it!

Earlier, ACIM teaches that the problem is not the world, which is neutral, but in how we perceive (project) the world. Therefore, in saving the world I am actually forgiving myself for the guilt-driven, unloving, and erroneous projection onto the world I made. In this way the world is saved by releasing it from the guilt I projected. Now I see the forgiven world through the eyes of Christ, instead of a sinful world through the ego's eyes of shame and fear. Also remember that the course uses the word *world* in two ways. One is the projected slaughterhouse world of pain, and the other is the *real world*.

What is the real world? The real world is not simply the same world we see now, except forgiven. Jesus gives us a hint:

> **Sit quietly and look upon the world you see, and tell yourself: "The real world is not like this. It has no buildings and there are no streets where people walk alone and separate. There are no stores where people buy an endless list of things they do not need. It is not lit with artificial light, and night comes not upon it. There is no day that brightens and grows dim. There is no loss. Nothing is there but shines, and shines forever." (T-13.VII.1:1-7)**

The real world is not like here. There are no roads, buildings, artificial lights, or stores where we buy *an endless list of things* we do not need, nor even want.

For clarity, when Jesus teaches about the new vision, seeing the world through the forgiving eyes of Christ, it does not mean that we are going to see a transformed world with the body's eyes. Rather, the vision of Christ is of the mind: *understanding and interpreting* what we see differently, according to right-minded thinking instead of wrong-minded thinking, and "looking" past the surface ego and body to the Holy Spirit within a dear sister's mind:

> Do not seek vision through your eyes, for you made your way
> of seeing that you might see in darkness, and in this you are
> deceived. Beyond this darkness, and yet still within you, is
> the vision of Christ, Who looks on all in light. Your "vision"
> comes from fear, as His from love. (T-13.V.9:1-3)

When we are purified of belief in guilt, we will no longer "see" a guilty
world. When the mind is ruled by Love, we will see only the loving.
Christ looks on all through an attitude of Love and Light. As students
of ACIM, we are learning to share His Vision.

Forgiveness of Yourself

The first section of Chapter Two begins with a description of false
forgiveness. Perhaps this teaching about the wrong way to forgive is
stronger here than anywhere else in ACIM:

> No gift of Heaven has been more misunderstood than has
> forgiveness. It has, in fact, become a scourge; a curse where
> it was meant to bless, a cruel mockery of grace, a parody
> upon the holy peace of God. Yet those who have not yet
> chosen to begin the steps of prayer cannot but use it thus.
> Forgiveness' kindness is obscure at first, because salvation
> is not understood, nor truly sought for. What was meant to
> heal is used to hurt because forgiveness is not wanted. Guilt
> becomes salvation, and the remedy appears to be a terrible
> alternative to life. (S-2.I.1:1-6)

Notice how Jesus describes this false form of forgiveness (which is
the usual and traditional understanding): *a scourge, a curse, a cruel
mockery of grace, a parody upon the holy peace of God.* False prayer is
compared to false forgiveness earlier in the first chapter of *The Song
Of Prayer: To ask for the specific is much the same as to look on sin and*

then forgive it. To first make sin real and then forgive it is the definition of false forgiveness.

No gift of Heaven is more misunderstood than the grace of true
forgiveness. And yet Jesus teaches that until we begin climbing the
ladder of prayer, false forgiveness is the only way we can forgive. Thus
does He teach the mutual support of prayer and forgiveness. In order
to practice true forgiveness, we willingly climb the ladder of prayer
and in order to climb the ladder of prayer, we willingly practice true
forgiveness. Both are necessary. Later in *The Song Of Prayer* Jesus
teaches the order of progression: first I forgive, then I pray. If the ego
wins this round and I choose guilt over salvation, what is the *remedy* that *appears to be a terrible alternative to life?* Death, or suicide.
Death is not a remedy to anything but can only *appear* as remedy in
the dream illusion.

The term *forgiveness-to-destroy* appears nine times in ACIM, and
only in *The Song Of Prayer*. In true forgiveness I do not first make the
offence real and then forgive it. Instead, I forgive myself for projecting
unconscious guilt onto another. In that forgiveness, I withdraw the
projection I made and thus free a sister from the guilt I laid on her.
In forgiving that way, I free myself as well. We are forgiven together,
or not at all. These are some of Jesus' strongest words about false forgiveness: *Forgiveness-to-destroy is death,* and *God's mercy becomes a
twisted knife.*

> **Forgiveness-to-destroy will therefore suit the purpose of
> the world far better than its true objective, and the honest
> means by which this goal is reached. Forgiveness-to-destroy
> will overlook no sin, no crime, no guilt that it can seek and
> find and "love." Dear to its heart is error, and mistakes loom
> large and grow and swell within its sight. It carefully picks
> out all evil things, and overlooks the loving as a plague; a
> hateful thing of danger and of death. Forgiveness-to-destroy
> is death, and this it sees in all it looks upon and hates. God's**

mercy has become a twisted knife that would destroy the holy
Son He loves. (S-2.I.2:1-6)

The gory details of forgiveness-to-destroy are described: it *will overlook
no sin, no crime, no guilt that it can seek and find.* This false forgiveness
seeks to find in anyone: *error, and mistakes loom large and grow and
swell within its sight. It carefully picks out all evil things.* False forgiveness looks on Love as if it were *a hateful thing of danger and of death.*

Next, Jesus teaches true forgiveness: *Do not see error. Do not make
it real.* The implications are significant to our ascent up the ladder
of prayer.

> Would you forgive yourself for doing this? Then learn that
> God has given you the means by which you can return to
> Him in peace. Do not see error. Do not make it real. Select
> the loving and forgive the sin by choosing in its place the face
> of Christ. How otherwise can prayer return to God? He loves
> His Son. Can you remember Him and hate what He created?
> You will hate his Father if you hate the Son He loves. For as
> you see the Son you see yourself, and as you see yourself is
> God to you. (S-2.I.3:1-10)

False forgiveness is an act of hate. This forgiveness-to-hate blocks prayer
from rising. There is no difference between hating God's Daughter and
hating the Father Who only loves His Daughter. If I do hate a sister, I
am also hating myself, because the sister I hate is part of me, and the
mirror which shows me my true Identity as Christ. In fact, without
this sister I am doomed to duality. We escape together or not at all. I
forgive myself for making this mistake of omission (not understanding that this Sister *is* Christ). Otherwise, prayer is hypocritical. As I
see a sister, so I see myself. God does not argue or oppose.

To forgive a sister is actually an illusion, because the sin I see in
her is actually my guilt hidden in the unconscious vault of the mind
that I projected onto her as a defense mechanism, meanwhile denying

the whole mess! But because I placed this secret guilt in a sister, that is where I forgive it: *Only in someone else can you forgive yourself, for you have called him guilty of your sins, and in him must your innocence now be found.*

> As prayer is always for yourself, so is forgiveness always given you. It is impossible to forgive another, for it is only your sins you see in him. You want to see them there, and not in you. That is why forgiveness of another is an illusion. Yet it is the only happy dream in all the world; the only one that does not lead to death. Only in someone else can you forgive yourself, for you have called him guilty of your sins, and in him must your innocence now be found. Who but the sinful need to be forgiven? And do not ever think you can see sin in anyone except yourself. (S-2.I.4:1-8)

Even though the idea of forgiving anyone is an illusion, it is *the only happy dream in all the world.* Both happy dreams and nightmares are temporary illusions. So here is the tricky, and important part to remember: if I see sin in anyone, I deny the Truth of sinlessness, and reinforce guilt, and prolong the separation. Jesus ends the paragraph with an important Truth: *do not ever think you can see sin in anyone except yourself.* What is it like to *not see error*?

Why is forgiveness of another an illusion? Because I do not forgive another; I forgive myself. Twice in the above quote Jesus presents his turnaround teaching about forgiveness that we looked at in the previous chapter. From the quote above: *It is impossible to forgive another, for it is only your sins you see in him. You want to see them there, and not in you.* Who is forgiveness for? Myself. What does a sister have to do with it? Because I tried to hide my guilt in her, that's where I find it, and forgive it. Why do I see my sins in my sister? Because I want to. I want to see sin in her instead of in me. This is the insane ego plan to escape guilt. Most of us learn the hard way that projection and denial do not bring peace.

The relatively recent psychological discovery of unconscious defense mechanisms, especially projection and denial, was necessary before ACIM could come. Whenever I see someone else as an enemy and having the power to attack and hurt me, I deceive myself and become slave to the world's weary ways. It is always somebody else who is bad, not me.

> **This is the great deception of the world, and you the great deceiver of yourself. It always seems to be another who is evil, and in his sin you are the injured one. How could freedom be possible if this were so? You would be slave to everyone, for what he does entails your fate, your feelings, your despair or hope, your misery or joy. You have no freedom unless he gives it to you. And being evil, he can only give of what he is. You cannot see his sins and not your own. But you can free him and yourself as well. (S-2.I.5:1-8)**

If I see anyone as an evil sinner, then she must be able to control how I feel. In that case, I am *the great deceiver of* myself. My fate, feelings, fear, despair or hope, misery or joy, are all determined by some secret, hated, and evil enemy, who controls me. I *think* I am slave to this evil sister who seems to be making me miserable. I forgot the truth that frees both her and I. Defensive devices are designed to deceive.

We will make mistakes while we walk the carpet of time, but *how* we interpret those mistakes is important. The deepest and most unconscious guilt secretly tells us that we are horrible sinners, and that we committed the most grievous sin of desiring to separate from God: the original sin, and worse, that we attempted to destroy God, and continue to do so. Jesus teaches us, instead, how to view all mistakes as *tiny shadows*. These shadows temporarily throw shade onto the face of Christ. How long these shadows hide the face of Christ in anyone is up to us. If we listen to Jesus, He teaches us how to make these shadows *quickly gone*.

Forgiveness, truly given, is the way in which your only hope of freedom lies. Others will make mistakes and so will you, as long as this illusion of a world appears to be your home. Yet God Himself has given all His Sons a remedy for all illusions that they think they see. Christ's vision does not use your eyes, but you can look through His and learn to see like Him. Mistakes are tiny shadows, quickly gone, that for an instant only seem to hide the face of Christ, which still remains unchanged behind them all. His constancy remains in tranquil silence and in perfect peace. He does not know of shadows. His the eyes that look past error to the Christ in you. (S-2.I.6:1-7)

My only hope for getting out of this mess is true forgiveness, combined with prayer. The metaphor of shade is interesting. Shade does not change what is shaded. Mistakes, large or small, *only seem to hide the face of Christ* for an instant...*His constancy remains.*

What is the God-Given remedy for all illusions of sin, guilt, fear, and separation? *Christ's vision*: seeing myself, everyone, and the world through the eyes of Christ. The forgiving eyes of Christ do not see the illusions of form by way of projection. Christ's vision is a loving attitude motivated by a knowledge of the Truth, not visual perception. Although we are aware of the mistakes we make, and judge ourselves as guilty, these tiny shadows are not recognized by Christ: *He does not know of shadows. His the eyes that look past error to the Christ in you.* We learn to understand as He does, looking past illusion to the Truth in everyone. That is putting on the Christ Mind.

To learn this shift from false forgiveness to true forgiveness, we ask for help. We ask Christ to teach us how to forgive like He does, how to understand like He does. We need His helping grace, and this schooling is so important that our *salvation rests on learning this from Him.*

Ask, then, His help, and ask Him how to learn forgiveness as His vision lets it be. You are in need of what He gives, and your salvation rests on learning this of Him. Prayer cannot be released to Heaven while forgiveness-to-destroy remains with you. God's mercy would remove this withering and poisoned thinking from your holy mind. Christ has forgiven you, and in His sight the world becomes as holy as Himself. Who sees no evil in it sees like Him. For what He has forgiven has not sinned, and guilt can be no more. Salvation's plan is made complete, and sanity has come. (S-2.I.7:1-8)

Prayer cannot rise to Heaven while we maintain the forgiveness that the world teaches: forgiveness-to-destroy. False forgiveness is *withering and poisoned thinking*, the ego's wrong-mindedness, that the Holy Spirit is purifying from our *holy* mind. God's mercy, extended through the Holy Spirit, removes this stinkin' thinkin' as we accept the Atonement Truth that everyone is already fully and truly forgiven. Smell no evil. See no evil. Hear no evil. Taste no evil. Touch no evil. Feel no evil. Think no evil. Speak no evil. Dream no evil. Imagine no evil. Remember no evil. Make no evil. Will no evil. When we are this way, we understand with Christ's vision. What kind of forgiveness do we learn? *...forgiveness as His vision lets it be.*

Course students are challenged to juggle two ways of being. One is seeing the innocence and sinlessness of everyone. The other is to be aware of the ego and its ways. Watching the ego is not finding fault with another. I watch the ego in myself. It is not easy, and it must be done without judgment, and joined together with Jesus or the Holy Spirit. I need this ego watching discipline so that I can make a different choice and join with the Holy Spirit instead of the ego. Looking in this way brings what is unconscious to what is conscious. If I do not look at the ego, it is protected.

> No one can escape from illusions unless he looks at them, for
> not looking is the way they are protected...The "dynamics"
> of the ego will be our lesson for a while, for we must look
> first at this to see beyond it, since you have made it real.
> (T-11.V.1:1;5)

Observing the ego is needed to notice its ways and deceptions, to learn that I no longer want it. The ego will resist this observation and try to prevent it with various distractions. It knows that I will renounce it, if I see what it actually is, and the suffering it maintains.

Instead of witnessing another's sin, I focus on the cringe-worthy thoughts and behavior of the self-made ego, as ugly and embarrassing as it may seem. Until we do this humble and honest observation, we will resist the Holy Spirit's assistance in deconstructing this special, separate self. When I see the ego for what it is, it is not difficult to relinquish. I will want to be rid of it. Jesus cannot join with anyone's ego because He renounced the ego in himself:

> When you unite with me you are uniting without the ego,
> because I have renounced the ego in myself and therefore
> cannot unite with yours. Our union is therefore the way to
> renounce the ego in you. The truth in both of us is beyond
> the ego. Our success in transcending the ego is guaranteed by
> God, and I share this confidence for both of us and all of us. I
> bring God's peace back to all His children because I received
> it of Him for us all. Nothing can prevail against our united
> wills because nothing can prevail against God's.
> (T-8.V.4:1-6)

I cannot join with Jesus and include the ego. In fact, recognizing that mind is already and always joined with Jesus' mind into the Christ Mind is the way I renounce ego. When any will is united with His will, great strength is gained: *Nothing can prevail against our united wills...* Who does Jesus bring peace to? All God's children. He received God's peace for us all. The Truth of Christ is We not me.

If I continue to see sin anywhere, I am insane, choosing hell over Heaven. This is the simple choice, the only choice. I see God's Daughter as either innocent or guilty. No compromise. We cannot be both innocent and guilty. They are mutually exclusive ideas. We are saved together, by offering salvation to each other, *by offering Christ's Love* to each other.

> **Forgiveness is the call to sanity, for who but the insane would look on sin when he could see the face of Christ instead? This is the choice you make; the simplest one, and yet the only one that you can make. God calls on you to save His Son from death by offering Christ's Love to him. This is your need, and God holds out this gift to you. As He would give, so must you give as well. And thus is prayer restored to formlessness, beyond all limits into timelessness, with nothing of the past to hold it back from reuniting with the ceaseless song that all creation sings unto its God. (S-2.I.8:1-6)**

Forgiveness is our need, and God's grace.

Up until the last sentence of the quote above, Jesus is teaching us how to think like Him in this dualistic world. The last sentence, a beautiful one, switches back to the non-dual level one. Forgiveness restores prayer to true prayer: *And thus is prayer restored to formlessness, beyond all limits into timelessness, with nothing of the past to hold it back from reuniting with the ceaseless song that all creation sings unto its God.* Why does the past hold back prayer? Because the past clips the wings of forgiveness with grudges and grievances, and the past holds all the ego's evidence for separation, sin, guilt, and fear: *You can hold on to the past only through guilt.* (T-13.I.8:2)

No past means no guilt. If I carry guilt I become stuck in the past trying to deal with karma and miss out on what the present, free of the past, offers everyone. *The ego invests heavily in the past, and in the end believes that the past is the only aspect of time that is meaningful.* (T-13.IV.4:2) We looked at the teaching about prayer and time in the previous chapter: *Prayer for specifics always asks to have the past repeated in some way* (S-1.IV.3:3) and the *aim of prayer is to release the present from its chains of past illusions...* (S-1.IV.3:5)

We learn to give forgiveness like God gives it. Even though the forgiveness God gives is unconditional, we can resist it. Who would rather look on sin than the face of Christ? The insane. Before we return to non-dual Heaven, we learn about the difference between true forgiveness and false forgiveness, or forgiveness-to-destroy. The term below, *Therefore we make distinctions*, explains how the Holy Spirit works with us in duality because there are no distinctions in Heaven. The language is deceptive because we are deceived.

> But to achieve this end you first must learn, before you
> reach where learning cannot go. Forgiveness is the key, but
> who can use a key when he has lost the door for which the
> key was made, and where alone it fits? Therefore we make
> distinctions, so that prayer can be released from darkness
> into light. Forgiveness' role must be reversed, and cleansed
> from evil usages and hateful goals. Forgiveness-to-destroy
> must be unveiled in all its treachery, and then let go forever
> and forever. There can be no trace of it remaining, if the plan
> that God established for returning be achieved at last, and
> learning be complete. (S-2.I.9:1-6)

We exchange false forgiveness for true forgiveness. In order to achieve this reversal, we learn to identify the many forms of false forgiveness and renounce them as false and tragic.

The paragraph above also begins a new teaching about forgiveness that Jesus will expand upon in the remainder of *The Song Of Prayer*: *Forgiveness is the key, but who can use a key when he has lost the door for which the key was made, and where alone it fits?* Despite all this teaching about the importance of forgiveness, we don't know what true forgiveness is, nor how to practice it.

In this dualistic world of opposites, we make the choice between forgiveness-to-destroy and true forgiveness *every instant*. This requires a level of discipline and diligence that I do not yet have. It is like asking an out-of-shape senior to run a marathon, today. She could not do it. But she might start out by walking a mile in a brother's sneakers, and gradually increase practicing. Practicing what? Practicing to remember the Truth.

> **This is the world of opposites. And you must choose between them every instant while this world retains reality for you. Yet you must learn alternatives for choice, or you will not be able to attain your freedom. Let it then be clear to you exactly what forgiveness means to you, and learn what it should be to set you free. The level of your prayer depends on this, for here it waits its freedom to ascend above the world of chaos into peace. (S-2.I.10:1-5)**

Without true forgiveness prayer *waits its freedom to ascend above the world of chaos into peace*. Jesus is teaching the alternative to false forgiveness and we need to learn *exactly what forgiveness means to you, and learn what it should be to set you free*. In this *world of opposites* I can choose to see a sister as opposed to me, and I need to *learn alternatives* to that mistake. We need to learn what forgiveness is in order to be free.

Forgiveness-to-Destroy

Now, *The Song Of Prayer* devotes a whole section of Chapter Two, eight paragraphs, to continuing a discussion of forgiveness-to-destroy, and the various forms it takes: *all its treachery*. Some forms are subtler and more secret than others. Jesus does not water down His teaching, nor sugar coat it: *Forgiveness-to-destroy* is identified and relinquished: *let go forever and forever*.

> Forgiveness-to-destroy has many forms, being a weapon of
> the world of form. Not all of them are obvious, and some are
> carefully concealed beneath what seems like charity. Yet all
> the forms that it may seem to take have but this single goal;
> their purpose is to separate and make what God created
> equal, different. The difference is clear in several forms where
> the designed comparison cannot be missed, nor is it really
> meant to be. (S-2.II.1:1-4)

Forgiveness-to-destroy is described above as a weapon *of the world of form*, and its single and only purpose is the opposite of true forgiveness, regardless of its many forms. Forgiveness-to-destroy is designed to separate us from God and everyone, and to prove that we are different from each other. One of us must be more sinful than the other, or holier than the other. Such is the fruit of separation and specialness. This may not be so obvious and might be disguised as charity.

In the next paragraph Jesus describes a most basic and blatant form of forgiveness-to-destroy. In this example, I who "forgave" actually consider myself superior to and more holy than the guilty sinner I stooped down to save. True forgiveness realizes that we are all the same and sinless as God created us. We join into one Child of God. Any form of forgiveness that promotes differences between us is false and deadly, confirming separation.

> In this group, first, there are the forms in which a "better"
> person deigns to stoop to save a "baser" one from what he
> truly is. Forgiveness here rests on an attitude of gracious
> lordliness so far from love that arrogance could never be
> dislodged. Who can forgive and yet despise? And who can
> tell another he is steeped in sin, and yet perceive him as
> the Son of God? Who makes a slave to teach what freedom
> is? There is no union here, but only grief. This is not really
> mercy. This is death. (S-2.II.2:1-8)

If I feel superior to the person I forgave, I can know that this is forgiveness-to-destroy and not true forgiveness. Jesus does not mince words here. This form of forgiveness-to-destroy reveals an *attitude of gracious lordliness so far from love that arrogance could never be dislodged.* I know I am in ego-mode whenever I see sin in anyone.

Steven Spielberg's *Schindler's List* is a significant film. Some scenes from that movie apply to this teaching. It's been a while since I viewed this black and white picture, so I am going on memory here. At one point, Schindler tricks the German officer in charge of a concentration camp in Poland during WWII. He appeals to the commander's ego, telling him that the power to pardon is greater than the power to kill. The officer took the bait and he started to see himself as even more superior than he already considered himself because he could pardon these people whom he used as sniper target practice, shooting children from his patio with a rifle. The practice of pardon did not last long though before the killing and torture continued. This film is a masterpiece and demonstrates how the Holy Spirit can take the darkest worldly situations and transform them into a classroom for holy liberation. The movie is really about the transformation Schindler experienced in that classroom. In addition, *Schindler's List* demonstrates both special and holy relationships.

Another form of forgiveness-to-destroy is when I consider myself to be a sinner too, not necessarily better, but I share sinfulness and guilt with everyone. In Catholic theology, everyone is born into the state of original sin. Automatically, before I take my first breath, I am a serious sinner doomed to hell. Apparently there is a way to avoid this fate but few find faith and most are not enjoying the ride as they travel the wide and welcoming highway to hell. Sharing sin might appear humble and true, but in fact it makes the same mistake as in any other form of false forgiveness, and that is the error of first making sin real, and then "forgiving" it. It does not matter who I accuse. Same mistake, *if it is understood.*

Another form, still very like the first if it is understood, does not appear in quite such blatant arrogance. The one who would forgive the other does not claim to be the better. Now he says instead that here is one whose sinfulness he shares, since both have been unworthy and deserve the retribution of the wrath of God. This can appear to be a humble thought, and may indeed induce a rivalry in sinfulness and guilt. It is not love for God's creation and the holiness that is His gift forever. Can His Son condemn himself and still remember Him? Here the goal is to separate from God the Son He loves, and keep him from his Source. (S-2.II.3:1-6;4:1)

In the quote immediately above I included the first sentence of the next paragraph (in *The Song Of Prayer*) as the last sentence of this paragraph, because it makes more sense to me. Dr. Wapnick himself pointed out paragraphing errors and described the process of proof reading *A Course In Miracles* as *tortuous*, which caused a chuckle. Although the form of ACIM is not perfect, the content is.

Jesus gives many examples to teach us how to identify and relinquish all forms of forgiveness-to-destroy. Can we condemn God's Daughter and still remember God? No. Can I condemn myself and still remember the Father? No. I remember a monastic story that demonstrates this idea of shared sinfulness. I think it was a desert father story but I don't remember exactly where I heard it. Here is a version from memory:

A sister and a hermit left their monastery and walked into a town to beg for their daily bread, as was their custom. They each went their own way to find food and then joined again later that day to walk back to the monastery. The hermit was upset because he felt so guilty for committing a serious and mortal sin while in town: fornication. Finally, unable to bear this guilty burden, he confessed his sin to his sister, and said he could not return to the monastery because of his shame. The sister, who was not tempted to sin while in town, told a white lie to her guilty brother hermit. She said something like this to her brother: "Brother, do not despair; I know how you feel. I did the same thing while in town. A handsome and horny young man invited me into his home, promising some delicious American cuisine. Then he dropped his robe and tempted me into his bed... I did not resist! I committed the same sin as you! Let us go back to the monastery together and confess our sins to Father Prior, and *then* we will be forgiven." And so that is what they did.

It might seem that the innocent sister was humble and loving to confess to an act she did not do, just to help her fellow brother. This form of forgiveness, cloaked as kind and humble, may actually produce a rivalry in sin and guilt! The ego wants to be first in everything, including sin. Me first expands into *my* gender first, *my* family first, *my* religion first, *my* race first, *my* country first, etc. Is the united states of unconsciousness number one in egoism? Here is progress: we develop from being egocentric, to being ethnocentric, to being world-centric, to being cosmos-centric, to eventually being Christo-centric, and include *everyone* under God's Infinite Tent.

Shared sinfulness is simply a disguised form of forgiveness-to-destroy, because it still sees sin as real. It is disguised as *charity* and appears as "loving." Anyone familiar with Christian, Jewish, or Muslim religions knows that their theologies emphasize the reality of sin, and eternal punishment in hell for sin, the justice and wrath of God. In other words, these religions are *sin-based, guilt-based, and fear-based*. These religions are exclusive because they exclude anyone who disagrees with the status quo, to the point of slow torture and murder. This is the opposite of what Jesus is teaching about forgiveness, sin, guilt, and fear. Jesus repeats over and over again in ACIM that we cannot bring fear into the Kingdom of Divine Love, and He warns about bringing fear into His teaching, as is what happened in Christianity. The Christian path, however, has the same outcome as ACIM, or any truth-seeking system, but it takes longer. The mistake of the sister above is the same mistake of all forms of forgiveness-to-destroy: first making sin real, and then acting in a *charitable* way and offering forgiveness. False forgiveness is the opposite of charity.

In the next example, Jesus talks about people who want to be martyrs. I believe it is, or was, a teaching in the Catholic Church that martyrdom leads to sainthood and Heaven. Some Christians saw this as a way of picking up their cross and following Jesus' example of dying on the cross in order to save us from our sins. They actually *tried* to get martyred. Martyrdom is the fast track to sainthood.

> This goal is also sought by those who seek the role of martyr at another's hand. Here must the aim be clearly seen, for this may pass as meekness and as charity instead of cruelty. Is it not kind to be accepting of another's spite, and not respond except with silence and a gentle smile? Behold, how good are you who bear with patience and with saintliness the anger and the hurt another gives, and do not show the bitter pain you feel. (S-2.II.4:2-5)

In seeking martyrdom, I pretend to suffer murder, or spite, willingly, but underneath I still feel bitter pain. In this case, spiritual special-ness is established as I feel superior to the people attacking me. Yet a veneer of meekness is dishonest denial and hides the rotten wood underneath the pretty surface, the sour honesty of how I really feel hurt. I make separation real because the killer and I must be different and I am the better one. This is the goal of every form of forgiveness to kill: divide and destroy. Don't murder me.

One of the challenges in identifying forgiveness-to-destroy is that it hides. Its cloaking system fools us. Hence Jesus is trying to teach us to recognize and identify all forms of false forgiveness so that we can notice them and abandon them. I must look at them and recog-nize them for what they are if I am going to be free of them. Without becoming aware of it and watching my use of forgiveness to kill, it does its deadly deals in secret, still unconscious.

Another form of pseudo-forgiveness is showing someone that I suffer. In this display of pain, I silently and irresponsibly blame another for how I feel. If I present a *face of suffering*, I am secretly, or not-so-secretly, accusing someone of causing this pain, even though on the surface I may claim forgiveness, and lay the lie that I do not blame you. Children do this all the time. They make mad faces to show how angry they are that usually say or shout, "You made me mad!" Adults tend to be subtler about it as they are generally more filtered and more calculative in what they show others.

> **Forgiveness-to-destroy will often hide behind a cloak like this. It shows the face of suffering and pain, in silent proof of guilt and of the ravages of sin. Such is the witness that it offers one who could be savior, not an enemy. But having been made enemy, he must accept the guilt and heavy-laid reproach that thus is put upon him. Is this love? Or is it rather treachery to one who needs salvation from the pain of guilt? What could the purpose be, except to keep the witnesses of guilt away from love? (S-2.II.5:1-7)**

In making this mistake of false forgiveness, I turn a sister into a secret enemy instead of what She truly is. In what She truly is, Her true Identity, lies the salvation that we share. Therefore, when I make anyone into an enemy, consciously or unconsciously, I deny liberation for both of us. This is a subtler form of false forgiveness. I may not consciously accuse you, but just demonstrating that I suffer *is silent proof of guilt and of the ravages of sin.*

Another form of forgiveness-to-destroy is a bartering form of forgiveness that is conditional. I will forgive you *if* you admit your offense and apologize. True forgiveness is unconditional: *God gives and does not ask for recompense.* Both sun and moon give their light away for free to everyone. Unconditional is one of the most challenging words for us because nothing here is unconditional as it is in Heaven.

> Forgiveness-to-destroy can also take the form of bargaining and compromise. "I will forgive you if you meet my needs, for in your slavery is my release." Say this to anyone and you are slave. And you will seek to rid yourself of guilt in further bargains which can give no hope, but only greater pain and misery. How fearful has forgiveness now become, and how distorted is the end it seeks. Have mercy on yourself who bargains thus. God gives and does not ask for recompense. There is no giving but to give like Him. All else is mockery. For who would try to strike a bargain with the Son of God, and thank his Father for his holiness? (S-2.II.6:1-10)

If I try to manipulate or intimidate a sister in exchange for "forgiveness" I am treating her like a slave I control. Then, in fact, I make myself a slave, because, Sisters-Я-Us. How I see anyone is how I see myself. If I bargain forgiveness, I get only *greater pain and misery* and make forgiveness *fearful*, the opposite of true forgiveness that removes fear because it removes guilt.

Forgiveness-to-destroy reinforces the guilt in my mind just because it keeps another guilty. Jesus calls it *pitiful* to misuse and distort forgiveness into *further slavery and pain*. If I use any form of forgiveness-to-destroy, consciously or unconsciously, I am choosing death and separation. True forgiveness leads to freedom, the opposite of slavery.

> What would you show your brother? Would you try to reinforce his guilt and thus your own? Forgiveness is the means for your escape. How pitiful it is to make of it the means for further slavery and pain. Within the world of opposites there is a way to use forgiveness for the goal of God, and find the peace He offers you. Take nothing else, or you have sought your death, and prayed for separation from your Self. Christ is for all because He is in all. It is His face forgiveness lets you see. It is His face in which you see your own. (S-2.II.7:1-9)

The above paragraph offers an advanced thought: *Christ is for all because He is in all.* True forgiveness permits us to see the sinless face of Christ in everyone. Jesus teaches earlier in the *Text: God is All in all in a very literal sense. All being is in Him Who is all Being. You are therefore in Him since your being is His.* (T-7.IV.7:4-6) We all dwell in God. True forgiveness is inclusive. Forgiveness-to-hate is exclusive.

Jesus asks us to be aware of what false forgiveness is, and aware of the fruit proving forgiveness false: if it leads to *anger, condemnation or comparisons of every kind*, then we can know that this is forgiveness-to-destroy which leads to death, not eternal life. True forgiveness leads *away* from comparisons, judgment, anger, and condemnation, which are deadly ego effects.

> **All forms forgiveness takes that do not lead away from anger, condemnation and comparisons of every kind are death. For that is what their purposes have set. Be not deceived by them, but lay them by as worthless in their tragic offerings. You do not want to stay in slavery. You do not want to be afraid of God. You want to see the sunlight and the glow of Heaven shining on the face of earth, redeemed from sin and in the Love of God. From here is prayer released, along with you. Your wings are free, and prayer will lift you up and bring you home where God would have you be.** (S-2.II.8:1-8)

Now why would Jesus teach that we want to *see the sunlight and glow of Heaven shining on the face of the earth* when He already declared, *There is no world*? The world can be a reflection of hell or Heaven. We can choose which version we want. The happy dream, still an illusion as is the world, is a gentler transition between this world and Heaven. I will explore this issue with similar course verses in the *Coda.*

Jesus is teaching us to see these forms of false forgiveness as *worthless in their tragic offerings* that lead to slavery and love-blocking fear. If we practice true forgiveness, prayer can rise to Heaven *with wings.* Prayer will lift us up and sing the whole home when prayer is released through forgiveness.

Forgiveness-for-Salvation

Now *The Song Of Prayer* spends a full section, seven paragraphs discussing Forgiveness-for-Salvation. The term, *Forgiveness-for-Salvation* appears only in *The Song Of Prayer*. Unlike forgiveness-to-destroy, with many different forms, Forgiveness for Salvation has *one form*:

> **Forgiveness-for-Salvation has one form, and only one. It does not ask for proof of innocence, nor pay of any kind. It does not argue, nor evaluate the errors that it wants to overlook. It does not offer gifts in treachery, nor promise freedom while it asks for death. Would God deceive you? He but asks for trust and willingness to learn how to be free. He gives His Teacher to whoever asks, and seeks to understand the Will of God. His readiness to give lies far beyond your understanding and your simple grasp. Yet He has willed you learn the way to Him, and in His willing there is certainty. (S-2.III.1:1-9)**

The above paragraph describes many characteristics of true forgiveness: it does not ask for evidence of innocence, nor seek any kind of payment, nor examine errors, nor argue, nor deceive with a façade of phony forgiveness, pretending to forgive but keeping a grudge. It might seem difficult to achieve true forgiveness, but it is not, because it is God's Will, and the Holy Spirit helps us. I simply will to forgive truly and set what were enemies free. The desire for forgiveness *is* the prayer for forgiveness. When she can fly free, so can I. As we shall see, *how* to forgive is not up to us. Who does God give His Teacher to? Anyone who asks sincerely seeking the Will of God.

In reading other course authors, one comes across various "forms" of true forgiveness and I offered a version in *God Is*. These are different ways to practice the one truth, leading to the same end: inclusive freedom from guilt. Sometimes students get confused about *how* to practice true forgiveness. The forms include a three-step process and realizing there is nothing to forgive in the first place. In the *Workbook*, the first *theme of special relevance* teaches answers to the question *What is Forgiveness?*

> Forgiveness recognizes what you thought your brother did to you has not occurred. It does not pardon sins and make them real. It sees there was no sin. And in that view are all your sins forgiven. What is sin, except a false idea about God's Son? Forgiveness merely sees its falsity, and therefore lets it go. What then is free to take its place is now the Will of God. (W-pII.1:1-7)

What is sin? Sin is a *false idea about God's Son.*

Another form of forgiveness-for-salvation is presented on the same page in the *Workbook:*

> Forgiveness, on the other hand, is still, and quietly does nothing. It offends no aspect of reality, nor seeks to twist it to appearances it likes. It merely looks, and waits, and judges not. He who would not forgive must judge, for he must justify his failure to forgive. (W-pII.1.4:1-4)

True forgiveness *is still, and quietly does nothing.* The form is not so important. Simply looking at the ego without judgment is a form of forgiveness. Sincere desire for forgiveness and the willingness that it be so, is the prayer of the heart for forgiveness, and that is enough. I do not know *how* it will come but I welcome it *however* it comes. Jesus teaches, with repetition, to leave the form of forgiveness to Him, or the Holy Spirit.

> Do nothing, then, and let forgiveness show you what to do, through Him Who is your Guide, your Savior and Protector, strong in hope, and certain of your ultimate success. (W-pII.1.5:1)

We do not choose the form of forgiveness and we do not do it: Do nothing until forgiveness shows us what to do.

In next few paragraphs of *The Song Of Prayer*, Jesus continues to teach a most advanced practice of true forgiveness: *not by your plans, but by His holy Will*. In the first line below, He uses the term *gifts of God*, which became the title of Helen Schucman's book of inspired poetry.

> **You child of God, the gifts of God are yours, not by your plans but by His holy Will. His Voice will teach you what forgiveness is, and how to give it as He wills it be. Do not, then, seek to understand what is beyond you yet, but let it be a way to draw you up to where the eyes of Christ become the sight you choose. Give up all else, for there is nothing else. When someone calls for help in any form, He is the One to answer for you. All that you need do is to step back and not to interfere. Forgiveness-for-Salvation is His task, and it is He Who will respond for you. (S-2.III.2:1-7)**

Do not, then, seek to understand what is beyond you yet... If we do not understand what true forgiveness is, how can we practice it? *Forgiveness-for-Salvation is His task*, not ours, yet we learn to share His vision. Who teaches what forgiveness really is and how to allow it *as He wills it be*? *His Voice*, which is the Holy Spirit. If someone asks for help, God's Voice, the Voice for God, provides the answer and all I do is *to step back and not to interfere*. If I interfere, I enter fear.

Forgiveness-for-salvation is the task of the Holy Spirit. If I try to do it myself, it is likely to backslide into forgiveness-to-destroy.

> **Do not establish what the form should be that Christ's forgiveness takes. He knows the way to make of every call a help to you, as you arise in haste to go at last unto your Father's house. Now can He make your footsteps sure, your words sincere; not with your own sincerity, but with His Own. Let Him take charge of how you would forgive, and each occasion then will be to you another step to Heaven and to peace. (S-2.III.3:1-4)**

Jesus teaches us not to choose the form of true forgiveness: *Let Him take charge of how you would forgive* and *do not establish what the form should be.* If I let the Holy Spirit or Jesus demonstrate true forgiveness, then I *arise in haste to go at last unto your Father's house.*

I make mistakes when I try to forgive because I cannot, yet, understand God's justice. These mistakes *still can be undone, for prayer is merciful.* But as the spiritual teeth, hidden and imprisoned in the spiritual gums, breakthrough and grow in understanding, I learn to chew the non-dual truth *that condemnation is not real* (S-2.III.4:5) because *condemnation is not of God* (T-8.VII.15:4).

> **Are you not weary of imprisonment? God did not choose this sorry path for you. What you have chosen still can be undone, for prayer is merciful and God is just. His is a justice He can understand, but you cannot as yet. Still will He give the means to you to learn of Him, and know at last that condemnation is not real and makes illusions in its evil name. And yet it matters not the form that dreams may seem to take. Illusions are untrue. God's Will is truth, and you are one with Him in Will and purpose. Here all dreams are done. (S-2.III.4:1-9)**

Only God's Will is true. The dream of duality ends when we know the truth that we are one with God in *Will and purpose.* The rest is illusion. The true humility that prayer brings allows us to confess honestly that we do not understand God nor the beatific blessing of true forgiveness: *His is a justice He can understand, but you cannot as yet.* The statement above, *it matters not the form that dreams may seem to take,* is another way of stating the first miracle principal. There is no order of difficulty in miracles because the form of illusions does not matter. They are all simply not true and the miracle recognizes this Truth. The miraculous solution to any and all forms of illusion is the same: a maximal expression of love.

What makes illusions in its evil name? Condemnation does this. I have not condemned anyone have I? Well, have I ever seen a sister as a body? Of course I have: *When you see a brother as a body, you are condemning him because you have condemned yourself.* (T-8.VII.15:7)

As usual in ACIM, Jesus repeats many of these ideas. He teaches again about the form of forgiveness: *let it not be you who sets the form in which forgiveness comes,* and, *Forgive him as the Christ decides you should.*

> "What should I do for him, Your holy Son?" should be the only thing you ever ask when help is needed and forgiveness sought. The form the seeking takes you need not judge. And let it not be you who sets the form in which forgiveness comes to save God's Son. The light of Christ in him is his release, and it is this that answers to his call. Forgive him as the Christ decides you should, and be His eyes through which you look on him, and speak for Him as well. He knows the need; the question and the answer. He will say exactly what to do, in words that you can understand and you can also use. Do not confuse His function with your own. He is the Answer. You the one who hears. (S-2.III.5:1-10)

It is a righteous relief that I do not choose the form of forgiveness, and I can leave that in the hands of the Holy Spirit or Christ. I simply desire God's Will for forgiveness, with willingness to accept whatever form the Holy Spirit chooses, and not interfere with ego. In this way I do not confuse human function with His function. We *need not judge* any form of seeking forgiveness.

ACIM teaches us not to judge forgiveness or choose the form it takes because *His forgiveness is not what you think it is.* In order to cooperate with forgiveness-for-salvation, Jesus teaches us to call on His Name and place the wish for forgiveness in His Hands. He is the Master Teacher of forgiveness and we are students of forgiveness.

Humility allows me to admit that forgiveness is not what I think it is. Since I don't know, I can yield to the Holy Spirit, Who does know.

> And what is it He speaks to you about? About salvation and the gift of peace. About the end of sin and guilt and death. About the role forgiveness has in Him. Do you but listen. For He will be heard by anyone who calls upon His Name, and places his forgiveness in His hands. Forgiveness has been given Him to teach, to save it from destruction and to make the means for separation, sin and death become again the holy gift of God. Prayer is His Own right Hand, made free to save as true forgiveness is allowed to come from His eternal vigilance and Love. Listen and learn, and do not judge. It is to God you turn to hear what you should do. His answer will be clear as morning, nor is His forgiveness what you think it is. (S-2.III.6:1-11)

By listening to His teaching, we learn how God, through Christ or the Holy Spirit, reverses forgiveness-to-destroy into forgiveness-for-salvation. We learn how He exchanges judgment and condemnation for true forgiveness. We learn that *Prayer is His Own right Hand* and this right Hand is free to save through true forgiveness. Who hears this Teacher? *Anyone who calls upon His Name, and places forgiveness in His hands.*

I learn to humbly accept that I do not know what true forgiveness is, while at the same time I accept that Jesus and the Holy Spirit do know what it is, and Their Knowing *should be enough.* We rest in our own not-knowing and trust His Knowing. The same teaching is given again using different words: *do not attempt to judge forgiveness, nor to set it in an earthly frame.*

> Still does He know, and that should be enough. Forgiveness has a Teacher Who will fail in nothing. Rest a while in this; do not attempt to judge forgiveness, nor to set it in an earthly

frame. Let it arise to Christ, Who welcomes it as gift to Him. He will not leave you comfortless, nor fail to send His angels down to answer you in His Own Name. He stands beside the door to which forgiveness is the only key. Give it to Him to use instead of you, and you will see the door swing silently open upon the shining face of Christ. Behold your brother there beyond the door; the Son of God as He created him. (S-2.III.7:1-8)

Earlier in *The Song Of Prayer* Jesus teaches that I have the key of forgiveness but I do not know what door it fits into. Now the Holy Spirit teaches us to give this key to Christ Who *stands beside the door to which forgiveness is the only key.* This final paragraph of the chapter on forgiveness offers much encouragement as well: *He will not leave you comfortless, nor fail to send His angels down to answer you in His Own Name,* and that the Teacher of forgiveness *will fail in nothing.*

This ends the chapter on forgiveness in *The Song Of Prayer*. The emphasis is on the relationship between prayer and forgiveness. Both are needed to ascend. Jesus teaches us to leave the form that forgiveness takes to the Holy Spirit. He also provides several examples of false forgiveness, including gracious lordliness so far from love it is arrogant, or, stooping to save, shared sinfulness, martyrdom, showing the face of suffering, and bartering for forgiveness. These different forms of false forgiveness share the same goal: to make sin and guilt real and sustain separation.

Here again, now gathered together, are Jesus' teachings about how to forgive, and how not to forgive, in the second chapter of *The Song Of Prayer*. We see how often he repeats Himself with different phrases in less than seven pages. I have added in brackets what the pronouns are referring to because the context is not included in these short quotes:

"...nor is His [God's] forgiveness what you think it is.

Do not establish what the form should be that Christ's forgiveness takes.

Let Him [Christ] take charge of how you would forgive...

...not with your own sincerity, but with His [Christ's] Own.

...not by your plans but by His [God's] holy Will.

His [God's] is a justice He can understand, but you cannot as yet.

And let it not be you who sets the form in which forgiveness comes...

Forgive him as the Christ decides you should...

Do not confuse His [Christ's] function with your own.

Forgiveness has been given Him [Christ] to teach, to save it from destruction...

...true forgiveness is allowed to come from His [God's] eternal vigilance and Love.

Rest a while in this; do not attempt to judge forgiveness, nor to set it in an earthly frame.

Give it [the key of forgiveness] to Him [Christ] to use instead of you...

Forgiveness-for Salvation is His [Christ's] task...

All that you need do is to step back and not interfere.

Do not, then, seek to understand what is beyond you yet...

Next, Jesus teaches about the relationship between prayer, forgiveness, and healing in the last chapter of *The Song Of Prayer*.

Chapter Four

PRAYER AND HEALING

*T*he third and final chapter in *The Song Of Prayer, Healing*, consists of a one paragraph *Introduction* and four sections: *The Cause of Sickness, False versus True Healing, Separation versus Union,* and *The Holiness of Healing*, a total of seven pages. The wealthy wisdom of *The Song Of Prayer* continues in its final chapter. The *Text, Workbook, Manual For Teachers*, and *Psychotherapy* offer further teaching about healing that dovetails with *The Song Of Prayer*. Because this is a long chapter, it is organized into nine sections, five of which correspond with the *Introduction* and four sections in *The Song Of Prayer*.

Introduction

Without some help, the ladder of prayer is steep, and climbing strenuous. With *both aids and witnesses*, however, the hard climb becomes gentler and surer. Other benefits of these aids and witnesses are described: *easing the pain of fear and offering the comfort and promises of hope.* What are these aids and witnesses that assist our ascent in prayer? They are healing and forgiveness. Jesus already explained the relationship between forgiveness and prayer. Prayer cannot rise above the bottom of the ladder without true forgiveness. Now He shifts the focus to the relationship between prayer, forgiveness, and healing. Healing is a *witness* to the power of forgiveness because it is an effect of forgiveness. Healing is also *aid* to prayer because healing gives *assurance of success in ultimate attainment of the goal.* Healing gives us confidence that God is true, and we are on the right path. The *Introduction* to *Healing*:

Prayer has both aids and witnesses which make the steep
ascent more gentle and more sure, easing the pain of fear and
offering the comfort and the promises of hope. Forgiveness'
witness and an aid to prayer, a giver of assurance of success
in ultimate attainment of the goal, is healing. Its importance
should not be too strongly emphasized, for healing is a sign
or symbol of forgiveness' strength, and only an effect or
shadow of a change of mind about the goal of prayer.
(S-3.in.1:1-3)

The importance of healing the body should not be over-emphasized,
however. Physical healing is an *effect* of true forgiveness, a shadow
or echo of the true healing in the mind. Healing is a *change of mind.*

The Cause of Sickness

One of the course's major teachings is about not confusing cause
and effect. In healing, we do not seek or pray for the effect of healing
the body, or symptoms of sickness. Rather, we pray for true healing.
True healing is of the mind, not the body. The removal of the belief
in guilt within the mind through forgiveness is the true healing. In
fact, guilt and sickness are so connected that they are one:

Herein is the release from guilt and sickness both, for they
are one. (M-3.II.3:11)

Guilt is not in the body. Guilt is in the mind. The mind is sick and the
body follows the mind like a shadow follows the body.

Healing is a *symbol of forgiveness' strength*, and, like forgiveness,
is temporary, useful in this dream world, but unneeded in Heaven,
where healing, forgiveness, and time are no more. Healing is one of
the echoes, or harmonics, of true forgiveness. We do not pray for the
echo; we pray the true song of thanksgiving and thank God for the

healing already given: our sins are forgiven; our mind is healed of its claim of guilt. Healing of the body is a temporary side effect, not the aim. However, if I identify with the body, and most of us do, then I will focus more on healing the body, including the brain, than the mind. One of the most repeated teachings in ACIM is about our Identity and how we are still as God created us. Jesus repeatedly stresses that the body/brain/personality is not our Identity. If I am more concerned with healing the body than healing the mind, then I am an *unhealed healer.* (T-9.V.1)

Earlier in the course Jesus gives the cause of sickness in three words: *sickness is separation* (T-11.II.1:1) and that in *the real world there is no sickness, for there is no separation and no division.* (T-11. VIII.10:1) The first paragraph of the first section on healing in *The Song Of Prayer* discusses the cause of sickness and warns us not to confuse cause (mind) and effect (body).

> **Do not mistake effect for cause, nor think that sickness is apart and separate from what its cause must be. It is a sign, a shadow of an evil thought that seems to have reality and to be just, according to the usage of the world. It is external proof of inner "sins," and witnesses to unforgiving thoughts that injure and would hurt the Son of God. (S-3.I.1:1-3)**

The cause and purpose of sickness will be described in several ways.

Jesus gives another example of the cause of sickness: *a shadow of an evil thought.* This evil thought is accepted by the world as true and just, but it is a lie, as are all evil thoughts. The ego is the father of lies. What is the evil thought causing the shadow of sickness, that hides the face of Christ? This wrong-minded idea is that sickness is *external proof of inner "sins."* This is a twisted and distorted view of sickness, the ego's view, the view that proves sin is real, and so is separation, and so is death. I try to mitigate God's ongoing punishment with the self-inflicted punishment of sickness. Because the dream of separation seems so sure, we resist remembering the truth. Remember the Gospel story where somebody asks Jesus whose sin caused a person's infirmity? It is an ancient ego belief.

Sickness also gives witness to *unforgiving thoughts that injure and would hurt the Son of God.* If I hold unforgiving thoughts, consciously or unconsciously, towards anyone, including myself, then I injure and hurt myself. I literally make myself sick and depressed by judging or condemning anyone. Soon Jesus will describe the cause of sickness as: *the sign of judgment made by brother upon brother.* Eventually, we will get sick and tired of judging and projecting grievous guilt onto others.

How did we get here? The belief in the original sin of separation produced a huge and unbearable belief in guilt. We try to escape our guilt by concealing it within the unconscious mind, and from there we project it onto the world and others. This shameful stain of guilt results in sickness and fear. It turns out that unconscious guilt is even worse than that caused by the wish to separate from God. After that, I wished to destroy God, and therefore Heaven, by usurping His throne and making myself cause and God an effect. I could not do this but I am insane enough to believe that I can, and did, do this.

If I consider the cause of sickness to be sin, I am reinforcing the ego's view of sickness and sin. In this case, I am actually preventing the healing of sickness by maintaining the guilt of sin. The wrong-minded thought system of the ego, that the world shares, trains our minds to believe that illusions are true from the day we got here. Healing is the result of the release from the mind's belief in guilt through true forgiveness. Not just the belief in sin and guilt, but the entire thought system of separation, which is ego's entire worldview. Hence we hesitate to heal.

Sickness is *not* punishment for sins by God. The belief that God is the just judge Who punishes people with illness and death only increases the fear of God, which sets one on the dark path leading away from Heaven. Thus, thinking that sin causes sickness is an *evil thought*, because it makes sin real, just like false forgiveness makes sin real. Therefore, if we want to be healed, and help in healing everyone, we first learn the true cause of sickness. If we do not understand this, then finding the cure is going to be difficult. Sickness itself is just an effect, not cause. The healer's focus is on healing cause, not healing effects.

No one can heal unless he understands what purpose sickness seems to serve. (W-pI.136.1:1)

Healing involves an understanding of what the illusion of sickness is for. Healing is impossible without this. (M-5.1:1-2)

Healers understand not only the cause but the purpose of sickness, which are similar and related. What is the purpose of sickness? Its purpose is as a defense against the truth, because illusions cannot stand in the light of truth. I fear losing the self-concept I made. I seem to prefer identity-confusion, and that is why I came here in the first place: to act a role and be what I am not. I am a pretender.

The ego intends to keep us in this darkness, hiding the true cause and purpose from us. It is a mistake to make sin the cause of anything because sin is not real. The *belief* in sin is strong though. Sickness does not have a true purpose; it only seems to have one in the sick and twisted ego plan, that we do not remember making, or agreeing to. In order to heal, I must remember the plan I laid and understand the purpose sickness seems to serve. *If* I understand the purpose of sickness, I can simply say, "I don't want this." And I am healed because I made a different choice. That is a big "if." (M-5.II.1:1-3)

So far there are three examples of the cause of sickness: separation, self-punishment for sin (or projected as divine punishment for sin), and judgment/condemnation of another. *Workbook* Lesson 136 gives more examples of the cause and purpose of sickness. It is not so much that there are many causes of sickness. There is one cause but several consequences of the primary cause of sickness: separation. Here is the sequence: the wish to separate from God produced severe guilt. The guilt produces fear of God's punishment. This fear blocks the awareness of love's presence. Because we lost our awareness of divine love, we need defense from this unloving God who is out to get us.

As Jesus teaches in a non-linear way, He approaches healing and sickness from many angles. In Lesson 136 our Teacher describes sickness as a *defense against truth* and a *decision* to be sick. ACIM is psychological as conservative psychology was in the late 60's. It is Freudian psychoanalytic not Jungian nor behavioral nor Rogerian or the plethora of psychologies developed since then. In particular Jesus uses psychoanalytic concepts of defense mechanisms and the unconscious mind. Projection and denial are well known and studied psychological defense mechanisms.

Yet here Jesus teaches that sickness and even making plans are defensive acts. He also teaches that I decided to be sick. This goes back to the major course teaching that I am responsible for everything that happens to me, including sickness and death.

> *I am responsible for what I see.*
>
> *I choose the feelings I experience, and I decide upon the goal I would achieve.*
>
> *And everything that seems to happen to me I ask for, and receive as I have asked.* (T-21.II.2:3-5)

This teaching of responsibility is easy to resist. I could not accept that I decided to be depressed. I hated being depressed. And it is unkind to tell someone who is hurting that her suffering is her own choice.

> **These patients do not realize they have chosen sickness. On the contrary, they believe that sickness has chosen them. Nor are they open-minded on this point. (M-5.III.1:6-8)**

Jesus understands our resistance to accepting responsibility for the mess we made.

In Lesson 136, Jesus explains how I made a decision to be sick, why I chose to be ill, and why I don't remember making any such request.

> **Sickness is not an accident. Like all defenses, it is an insane device for self-deception. And like all the rest, its purpose is to hide reality, attack it, change it, render it inept, distort it, twist it, or reduce it to a little pile of unassembled parts. The aim of all defenses is to keep the truth from being whole. The parts are seen as if each one were whole within itself. (W-pI.136.2:1-5)**

Defenses fragment the whole into parts and then consider a part to be whole in itself, which it cannot be in truth. Each part contains the whole, yet the whole includes every part, down to the smallest grain of sand. When I consider a separate self to be the whole, I make a mistake, and believe I am cause, instead of effect. Defenses defend the separation so that I can continue being special me, with a special body, the hero of the dream. What is the purpose of defense devices among which sickness is one? The purpose is *self-deception* and to *hide reality* by fragmenting the whole into pieces and hiding guilt in the unconscious, where it does its projection damage in darkness, like a movie theater needs to be dark for us to see the projected film...I seem unaware of what happened because it is intended to deceive. What happened to Humpty Dumpty?

Imagine you are in a theater and watching a movie. Suddenly all the lights come on in the room. Now the projected film cannot be seen. So we boo and complain to the manager about the light that is ruining the movie. Turn the lights off and now the images can be seen. We can choose lights on or lights off, but projection needs darkness for sleepy dreaming.

Jesus gives a rare teaching here about how I chose sickness, but do not remember doing so. If I did make a decision for sickness, then that decision was made unconsciously, right? Here He says that no, that decision was not unconscious but conscious. I sure don't remember making a decision to be depressed. And if I did, why would I? These questions are answered in this lesson.

> Defenses are not unintentional, nor are they made without awareness. They are secret, magic wands you wave when truth appears to threaten what you would believe. They seem to be unconscious but because of the rapidity with which you choose to use them. In that second, even less, in which the choice is made, you recognize exactly what you would attempt to do, and then proceed to think that it is done. (W-pI.136.3:1-4)

Decisions for sickness seem to be unconscious only because I forget about it immediately, less than one second after I made the decision: *because of the rapidity with which you choose to use them. Them* are the defenses I use to defend myself as an independent individual (ego). Sickness is one of these defenses.

> Who but yourself evaluates a threat, decides escape is necessary, and sets up a series of defenses to reduce the threat that has been judged as real? All this cannot be done unconsciously. But afterwards, your plan requires that you must forget you made it, so it seems to be external to your own intent; a happening beyond your state of mind, an outcome with a real effect on you, instead of one effected by yourself. (W-pI.136.4:1-3)

Because of this rapid forgetting, I can blame sickness on some external source, and fall into many other errors, such as sickness is punishment for sin, or blaming a sister. Since your mistake made me miserable, I condemn you and demand that we be separated and you be punished for hurting me. You offend me! Lock her up!

I could not make these false accusations without forgetting that I made the decision for sickness in the first place, a perfectly purposeless plan to plead you guilty. The purpose of sickness is described twice. First in the quote above: *defenses are secret, magic wands you wave when truth appears to threaten what you would believe.* And then in the quote below: *sickness is a choice you make, a plan you lay, when for an instant truth arises in your own deluded mind, and all your world appears to totter and prepare to fall. Now are you sick, that truth may go away and threaten your establishments no more.* Knowing the purpose of sickness shows why I decided to be sick. Sickness is a magic wand I wave when Truth threatens my self-concept and worldview, both based on belief in separation.

> **It is this quick forgetting of the part you play in making your "reality" that makes defenses seem to be beyond your own control. But what you have forgot can be remembered, given willingness to reconsider the decision which is doubly shielded by oblivion. Your not remembering is but the sign that this decision still remains in force, as far as your desires are concerned. Mistake not this for fact. Defenses must make facts unrecognizable. They aim at doing this, and it is this they do. (W-pI.136.5:1-6)**

Therefore, if I deceive and perceive myself as sick and do not remember that I asked for this, it means that the decision to be sick is still in place: *this decision still remains in force.* I can remember that I did this when I am willing to *reconsider the decision which is doubly shielded by oblivion.* Defenses *make facts unrecognizable,* by design. Sickness is not a fact. Defense is an illusion; I do not need any defense. In addition, what I am defending myself from, an angry, vindictive god, or another ego, adds illusion to illusions. Oblivion obscures decision.

> **Sickness is a decision. It is not a thing that happens to you, quite unsought, which makes you weak and brings you suffering. It is a choice you make, a plan you lay, when for an instant truth arises in your own deluded mind, and all your**

world appears to totter and prepare to fall. Now are you sick, that truth may go away and threaten your establishments no more. (W-pI.136.7:1-4)

Although Jesus teaches that *sickness is a decision* I made to be sick, it is hard for me to accept that, and I am not open-minded about it. He is explaining to anyone interested, the dynamics of sickness and healing that were pretty much secret, or unknown, before He gave us ACIM.

In the *Psychotherapy* pamphlet Jesus confirms that sickness is a decision that is made through judgment because judgment is a decision:

> As all therapy is psychotherapy, so all illness is mental illness. It is a judgment on the Son of God, and judgment is a mental activity. Judgment is a decision, made again and again, against creation and its Creator. It is a decision to perceive the universe as you would have created it. It is a decision that truth can lie and must be lies. What, then, can illness be except an expression of sorrow and of guilt? (P-2.IV.1:1-6)

All illness is mental illness. In our society mental illness carries a stigma that physical illnesses do not share. But according to the course, diabetes, migraines, or broken bones are all mental illnesses. How so? Because they are all decisions in the mind.

> Once God's Son is seen as guilty, illness becomes inevitable. It has been asked for and will be received. And all who ask for illness have now condemned themselves to seek for remedies that cannot help, because their faith is in the illness and not in salvation. There can be nothing that a change of mind cannot effect, for all external things are only shadows of a decision already made. (P-2.IV.2:1-4)

I appreciate the consistency of teaching about the cause and effect connection between guilt and sickness throughout the whole course.

Jesus uses an interesting shadow metaphor here. Sickness is a shadow of a sick decision already made. How does one change a shadow? The only way to change a shadow is to change what is making the shadow. Let us say I am outside on a sunny day and I can see my shadow. If my ex went up and tried to destroy my shadow she could not do it. She could scream obscenities at it. She could jump up and down on it. She could shoot it with a 12-gauge shotgun at close range. She could throw gasoline on it and set it on fire. No matter what she did, it would not feel anything nor change because it is nothing. I can change the shadow by changing my position, turning, or sitting. The shadow just follows what it shadows. Sickness is a shadow. Sickness is not cured by healing the shadow. Sickness is healed by healing what caused the shadow: a decision in the mind. Change the decision and the shadow changes.

Sickness only happens because in the dream confusion we see some value in it, even though we might not admit believing this. That is why we chose it and that is why we must learn that sickness is not valuable, in order to make a different choice. We value sickness as a defense, but immediately forget the fact that being sick is part of the plan.

Healing must occur in exact proportion to which the valuelessness of sickness is recognized. (M-5.II.1:1)

Yet again, if I do not understand the purpose of pain, true healing is delayed. The basis for healing in all forms is the *acceptance of sickness as a decision of the mind*. Then I can change this decision. How will I change that decision if I do not understand that I made the decision in the first place?

The acceptance of sickness as a decision of the mind, for a purpose for which it would use the body, is the basis of healing. And this is so for healing in all forms. A patient decides that this is so, and he recovers. (M-5.II.2:1-3)

Think how different this approach is to the world's view of healing. If I went to a neuro-surgeon with brain cancer, the doctor would consider the body/brain to be sick, not the mind, and would treat the body. The brain cancer is only a shadow of the guilt cancer in the mind that needs healing to be gone. True healers treat cause, not symptoms.

Jesus teaches that only the mind needs healing because only the mind made the mad decision for sickness; only the mind decides for attack via judgment.

> **First, it is obvious that decisions are of the mind, not of the body. If sickness is but a faulty problem-solving approach, it is a decision. And if it is a decision, it is the mind and not the body that makes it. The resistance to recognizing this is enormous, because the existence of the world as you perceive it depends on the body being the decision maker. (M-5.II.1:4-7)**

The body does not choose anything, and is neutral, not bad, not good. This shift in perception, that puts cause and effect in their true sequence, is the only requirement for healing. The plan to use sickness as a problem-solving defense is faulty, and a decision I am responsible for. Whenever I make a poor decision, I have the option, and responsibility, to choose again. Why is the resistance to understanding that sickness is a choice so enormous? Because when I see the truth about sickness, my whole world view collapses; the walls of guilt come tumbling down.

> **What is the single requisite for this shift in perception? It is simply this; the recognition that sickness is of the mind, and has nothing to do with the body. (M-5.II.3:1-2)**

With this shift, however, comes a cost I may not be willing to pay: the end of self-concept and the end of the world.

What does this recognition "cost"? It costs the whole world
you see, for the world will never again appear to rule the
mind. (M-5.II.3:3-4)

Defenses kick in when I don't want to pay that cost: *the whole world
you see*. Before healing happens, I seem to be a victim of the world.
The body that is part of self-concept is subject to whatever spears the
world shakes at us: difficulties, devils, diseases, disasters, disabilities,
destructions, depressions, despairs, and deaths, in a word: drama. One
defense against this is to get sick. This goes back to identity-confusion
and body-identification:

Yet to accept this release, the insignificance of the body must
be an acceptable idea. (M-5.II.3:12)

The course is training our minds to a new perception of self and everyone. Slowly, slowly I let go of identifying as a body, with help from
the Comforter, Who is in charge of the deconstruction of me, at my
request and with my permission, willingness, and defenselessness.
Regarding this undoing of self-concept, I learn to welcome the Holy
Spirit's demolition derby and pray: *Make it so, Lord, make it so.* And
mean what I pray.

Continuing with Lesson 136, Jesus explains how sickness serves
as a planned defense against the truth:

How do you think that sickness can succeed in shielding
you from truth? Because it proves the body is not separate
from you, and so you must be separate from the truth. You
suffer pain because the body does, and in this pain are you
made one with it. Thus is your "true" identity preserved,
and the strange, haunting thought that you might be
something beyond this little pile of dust silenced and stilled.
For see, this dust can make you suffer, twist your limbs and
stop your heart, commanding you to die and cease to be.
(W-pI.136.8:1-5)

The purpose of sickness is as a defense against the truth of our Identity. Sickness is evidence that "proves" our bodies are real and our "true" identity as individual physical beings is preserved. Since I can experience physical pain, the physique must be real. The same is true about pleasure. Both pain and pleasure emphasize body-identification. Here Jesus describes the hard part about being a body: *this dust can make you suffer, twist your limbs, and stop your heart.* When I die as a dusty body, I cease to be. How does Jesus describe the body? It is *a little pile of dust.*

> **Thus is the body stronger than the truth, which asks you live, but cannot overcome your choice to die. And so the body is more powerful than everlasting life, Heaven more frail than hell, and God's design for the salvation of His Son opposed by a decision stronger than His Will. His Son is dust, the Father incomplete, and chaos sits in triumph on His throne. (W-pI.136.9:1-3)**

The above quote describes the insane ego plan of defense against the truth: *Such is your planning for your own defense.* (W-pI.136.10:1)

In truth, I am not sick; sickness is an illusion. I can only think that I am sick, and believe that defenses are working, even if they are not:

> **You can but choose to think you die, or suffer sickness or distort the truth in any way. What is created is apart from all of this. Defenses are plans to defeat what cannot be attacked. What is unalterable cannot change. (W-pI.136.11:4-7)**

Jesus is sharing an important truth in nine words: *What is created is apart from all of this.* All of this world of separation, sin, guilt, fear, suffering, sickness, and death, is apart from what God creates. If God created this battlefield world, then God must be an insane sadist. This world was not created by God. It was made by us, to be a place where we can hide out from God, be our own boss, and cherish guilt as we blame each other for sin and suffering. Remember how Eve and Adam tried to hide from God, and God pretends that He does not know where they are? We try to hide from God because we are afraid of Him and His punishment because of guilt, just like A & E. The quote below is interesting in terms of Christian theology:

> If this were the real world, God *would* be cruel. For no Father could subject His children to this as the price of salvation and *be* loving. *Love does not kill to save.* If it did, attack would be salvation, and this is the ego's interpretation, not God's. Only the world of guilt could demand this, for only the guilty could conceive of it. Adam's "sin" could have touched no one, had he not believed it was the Father Who drove him out of Paradise. For in that belief the knowledge of the Father was lost, since only those who do not understand Him could believe it. (T-13.in.3:1-7)

Love does not kill to save. Amen Brother J. Testify to the Truth! This is the True Testament. If this is the real world, what would God be? Cruel. Then we come up with blaming excuses and projecting guilt. Eve blames the snake. Adam blames Eve. Cain blames Able and what an imaginary mess we have now. Can you imagine how guilty Cain felt after killing his brother? The devil made us do it!

Our true Identity cannot be attacked and is *unalterable*. These dumb defenses will disappear when we are willing to accept the truth of our Identity:

> Truth has a power far beyond defense, for no illusions can remain where truth has been allowed to enter. And it comes to any mind that would lay down its arms, and cease to play with folly. It is found at any time; today, if you will choose to practice giving welcome to the truth. (W-pI.136.14:1-3)

When I lay down defenses, I can welcome the truth. What mind does truth come to? Any mind, any time, even today! When I do this, not how I do this, is up to me. When will I lay down my defenses and cease playing with folly? Today? Whenever I get tired enough of being sick and tired.

Then Jesus teaches us a prayer He calls the *healing prayer*, which is the exercise portion of this lesson. This *healing prayer* is the invitation to the truth of our Identity to return to what It never left:

> And truth will come, for it has never been apart from us.
> It merely waits for just this invitation which we give today.
> We introduce it with a healing prayer, to help us rise above
> defensiveness, and let truth be as it has always been:
>
> *Sickness is a defense against the truth. I will accept the
> truth of what I am, and let my mind be wholly healed today.*
> (W-pI.136.15:3-7)

Sickness is one form of defense against the truth of What-I-Am. When I drop defenses and welcome the truth of Christ Identity, the mind can be *wholly healed*. Only false healing is partial. True healing is complete and whole. What truth do I accept? *I will accept the truth of what I am.* Today, if I so choose. The usual caveat applies: it is one thing to say the words and it is another to mean them.

Next, Jesus gives us another radical teaching. This is how I know that I have dropped defenses and accepted the truth of spiritual Identity:

> Now is the body healed, because the source of sickness has
> been opened to relief. And you will recognize you practiced
> well by this: The body should not feel at all. If you have been
> successful, there will be no sense of feeling ill or feeling well,
> of pain or pleasure. No response at all is in the mind to what
> the body does. Its usefulness remains and nothing more.
> (W-pI.136.17:1-5)

When I realize that I am a mind/spirit and not a body/ego, I won't feel physical pain or pleasure. Yet the body remains useful for communication with everyone. This revolutionary teaching continues:

> Perhaps you do not realize that this removes the limits you
> had placed upon the body by the purposes you gave to it. As
> these are laid aside, the strength the body has will always be
> enough to serve all truly useful purposes. The body's health
> is fully guaranteed, because it is not limited by time, by
> weather or fatigue, by food and drink, or any laws you made
> it serve before. You need do nothing now to make it well, for
> sickness has become impossible. (W-pI.136.18:1-4)

I limit the body to suffering and death because of the purpose I gave
it: a container to hold my mind apart from everyone else and God.
As I uncover and let go of these special purposes, the body will be
healthy and sickness *becomes impossible.* The body will not be limited
by time (age), weather, fatigue, food and drink, or any of the laws I
made it serve. I don't know about you, but this effect of mind healing
sounds pretty good to me. I do not mind letting go of pleasure if it
means I can let go of suffering as well. (More on this later.)

> Yet this protection needs to be preserved by careful
> watching. If you let your mind harbor attack thoughts,
> yield to judgment or make plans against uncertainties to
> come, you have again misplaced yourself, and made a bodily
> identity which will attack the body, for the mind is sick.
> (W-pI.136.19:1-2)

Apparently, not feeling pain or pleasure in the body *needs to be preserved* by carefully watching the mind for any attack thoughts that
linger, or judgments I make, or even making *plans against uncertain-
ties to come.*

Without this mind-watching diligence I can easily fall back into
body-identification and defensiveness. Bodies do need defense because
they are used for attack. Because all thought produces form, we need
to be careful, and watch our mind. Thought supported by belief can

be more dangerous than an atomic bomb. Jesus presents his teaching about how powerful the mind is early in the course:

> Few appreciate the real power of the mind, and no one
> remains fully aware of it all the time. However, if you
> hope to spare yourself from fear there are some things you
> must realize, and realize fully. The mind is very powerful,
> and never loses its creative force. It never sleeps. Every
> instant it is creating. It is hard to recognize that thought
> and belief combine into a power surge that can literally
> move mountains...There are no idle thoughts. All thinking
> produces form at some level. (T-2.VI.9:3-8;13-14)

What is the power surge that can *literally* move Denali to Denver? The combination of *thought and belief.* Thoughts are creative only if we believe them. What kind of thoughts do not exist? *Idle thoughts.* Since all thought produces form, I learn to guard the mind. What forms do attack thoughts produce? One is terror.

> I cannot let you leave your mind unguarded, or you will not
> be able to help me. Miracle working entails a full realization
> of the power of thought in order to avoid miscreation.
> (T-2.VII.2:1-2)

I am responsible for what I believe. I learn to stop miscreating with a powerful but undisciplined mind and not depend on Jesus or the Holy Spirit to guard my thoughts for me:

> If I intervened between your thoughts and their results, I
> would be tampering with a basic law of cause and effect; the
> most fundamental law there is. I would hardly help you if
> I depreciated the power of your own thinking. This would
> be in direct opposition to the purpose of this course. It is
> much more helpful to remind you that you do not guard your
> thoughts carefully enough. (T-2.VII.1:4-7)

Here is a pretty tough spiritual discipline. I constantly receive thoughts. Their source is either ego or Holy Spirit. Whichever thoughts I choose to believe become my thoughts, with power to create or condemn, depending on the thought system I embrace. Mind chooses which thoughts to believe. Mind is the decision maker.

Jesus is reminding us about the power of Mind and if He or the Holy Spirit intervened between our chosen thoughts and their results, we would never learn this fundamental lesson. Mind is the cause that produces effects. Jesus will not interfere with the karmic law of cause and effect by intervening between our thoughts and their effects. Hence, He advises us to preserve protection by *carefully watching* our potent mind. If every thought immediately took form and became true, imagine how careful we would need to be to prevent miscreating.

Jesus teaches that purification is necessary before performing miracles in the seventh miracle principal on the first page of the *Text*. The non-duality of One Will is the only way to avoid miscreating conflict with an undisciplined and unwatched mind. What watches mind? Mind watches mind in the mind mirror, like the eyeball sees itself. Not really itself, but an image reflected in the polished glass. We watch our mind in the present to see which thoughts we are choosing to believe and give creative power to.

The last dangerous defense mentioned above, about making plans, is another radical teaching of Jesus. Making plans is another form of defense based on fear. This teaching is more fully explained in the *Workbook* lesson immediately preceding Lesson 136:

> **A healed mind does not plan. It carries out the plans that it receives through listening to wisdom that is not its own. It waits until it has been taught what should be done, and then proceeds to do it. It does not depend upon itself for anything except its adequacy to fulfill the plans assigned to it. It is secure in certainty that obstacles can not impede its progress to accomplishment of any goal that serves the greater plan established for the good of everyone.**

A healed mind is relieved of the belief that it must plan...
(W-pI.135.11:1-5;12:1)

What is the greater plan for the *good of everyone*? It is the Atonement. Jesus uses the words all and everyone frequently because the Atonement is unconditional and inclusive.

The mind engaged in planning for itself is occupied in setting
up control of future happenings. (W-pI.135.15:1)

Why would I want to control future happenings? Because I do not trust God.

The mind that plans is thus refusing to allow for change.
(W-pI.135.16:1)

Instead of making plans, I allow for change. Why would I refuse to allow for change? Because I do not trust God.

We will anticipate that time [when I am defenseless] today
with present confidence, for this is part of what was planned
for us. We will be sure that everything we need is given us
for our accomplishment of this today. We make no plans for
how it will be done, but realize that our defenselessness is all
that is required for the truth to dawn upon our minds with
certainty. (W-pI.135.21:1-3)

Defenselessness is like willingness, it *is all that is required* from me. Defenselessness is not doing anything. Defending a self-concept is doing something and interfering with the Holy Spirit's undoing of that unreal self. This defense tragically extends the time of suffering because it forces the Holy Spirit to wait for willingness and defenselessness. She does not oppose, force anything, nor try to control.

If I defend myself, it means I believe there is a real attack from which I need defense. The *folly of defense gives illusions* of attack *full reality.* (W-pI.135.1:2) Attack cannot happen, it is only an illusion; yet defensiveness only adds another illusion to the first (attack) making correction *doubly difficult*. When we do give in to any of these temptations to be defensive with planning, judging, projection, denial, or sickness, Jesus teaches us to *Give instant remedy* by dropping defenses. Defenselessness invites truth to replace identity-confusion. Is not a worried mind always on the look out for danger and scheming ways to protect itself or what it desires? How valuable is defense in this world? Trillions of dollars claimed for defense that is actually used for offence. Defense led to all weapons of war and they are used to kill, in the name of defense. If we really valued Peace, it might occur to us to replace departments of war and destruction with departments of peace and construction. Because we have inner conflict we have external conflict. War happens when war is within. To the Holy Spirit, however, war is just another classroom that She can use for liberation.

Give instant remedy, should this occur, by not allowing your defensiveness to hurt you longer. Do not be confused about what must be healed, but tell yourself:

I have forgotten what I really am, for I mistook my body for myself. Sickness is a defense against the truth. But I am not a body. And my mind cannot attack. So I can not be sick. (W-pI.136.20:1-7)

What have I forgotten? What I really am. Jesus hammers this idea of Identity repeatedly. I am not a body.

Today, in most "wholistic" and new age thought regarding wellness, the body is included. Body, Mind, Spirit is their mantra, as it was mine before there was Help on the way. ACIM is clearly different. The problem is not the body, but identifying as a body. Defenses, designed to protect the autonomous self, have a painful side effect:

Perhaps you have misunderstood His plan, for He would never offer pain to you. But your defenses did not let you

**see His loving blessing shine in every step you ever took.
(W-pI.135.18:2-3)**

When I try to defend myself, ironically, I hurt myself because these defenses block awareness of God's blessings. I do not need defenses, but illusions do.

In *The Song Of Prayer*, Jesus is teaching us what true healing is: mind healing that permits us to know our shared, true Identity, and this healing has other important benefits, like pure joy and a peaceful, gentle death.

> **Healing the body is impossible, and this is shown by the brief nature of the "cure." The body yet must die, and so its healing but delays its turning back to dust, where it was born and will return. (S-3.I.1:4-5)**

In the quote above, Jesus says that *Healing the body is impossible.* And then eight sentences later He says, the *body can be healed.* What? How can He contradict himself like that? Is Jesus using deceptive language? Misunderstanding this, misinterpreting it, can leave students confused and discouraged. Here is a good example of why I might slow down and carefully study the course. This is also a case in point demonstrating a challenge that course students face. We learn to hold both these ideas: healing the body is impossible, *and*, the body can be healed, as true. One is a relative truth and one is an absolute truth. Again, level confusion is the problem, solved with careful study. The first statement, *healing the body is impossible,* is a level one, non-dual teaching. Healing the body is impossible because the body is an effect, not cause, and the body is not real. Illusions are not healed; illusions disappear into the star dust from which they came.

Furthermore, this passage goes on to say that any so-called healing of the body is temporary because the body is going to die anyway. The body's healing is not true because it is limited and partial. The *brief nature of the "cure"* proves that the healing is not true. Everything that is temporary is temporal and part of the dream, not real, apart from What Is. Even if a healer facilitates or accepts a miraculous physical healing, the *body yet must die, and so its healing but delays its turning back to dust, where it was born and will return.* So, if I identify as a body this is what I can look forward to: a return to dust. However, on level two (duality), *the body can be healed.*

If I identify as a body, then I will fear death. The body will age, weaken, become sick, suffer pain, and die.

> **The body's cause is unforgiveness of the Son of God. It has not left its source, and in its pain and aging and the mark of death upon it this is clearly shown. Fearful and frail it seems to be to those who think their life is tied to its command and linked to its unstable, tiny breath. Death stares at them as every moment goes irrevocably past their grasping hands, which cannot hold them back. And they feel fear as bodies change and sicken. For they sense the heavy scent of death upon their hearts. (S-3.I.2:1-6)**

Here on earth healing can be true or false depending on whether the healing heals effect or cause, body/brain or mind. What causes the body? *Unforgiveness.*

We made the body to separate us. Bodies are separate and separation causes sickness. We all know what happens to the body, especially as the body ages and sickens. The accurate descriptions of the body and its fate continue: I seem *fearful and frail* if I identify with it because then I am identified with *its unstable, tiny breath. Death stares at them as every moment goes irrevocably past their grasping hand...they feel fear as bodies change and sicken. For they sense the heavy scent of death upon their hearts.* As dreadful as this description of the body and body-identification is, it is fairly easy to see the truth of what Jesus is teaching. Is it not true that anyone of us is one heartbeat away from death? Any breath could be my last. This talk of death, as the world views it, is setting the stage for His wonderful teaching about what a holy death is.

Another major course teaching related to identity, with much repetition, is that *ideas leave not their source.* This is primary to learning right-mindedness, and the truth of the Atonement. We are the creation of God, the extension of God's Love. As such, we are an effect of God that does not, and even cannot, leave Him, the Cause of all being. This is the divine design. All being is in Him. Where would I go? There is nowhere to go to. There is nothing outside of God. Even though ontologically we are still as God created us, we dream a nightmare that we are not, and in fact, we believe the ego's lie that we are so sinful that we deserve sickness as punishment in this world, while hoping that past and present infirmities might mitigate future hell in the next. The body, the effect or idea of the ego, does not leave its source as well (ego/death) and the proof is: *in its pain and aging and the mark of death upon it this is clearly shown.* Identifying as a body is choice for death, not life.

The ego *is* unforgiveness, and Jesus teaches that the body is a physical manifestation of the ego:

> **The ego's fundamental wish is to replace God. In fact, the ego is the physical embodiment of that wish. For it is that wish that seems to surround the mind with a body, keeping it separate and alone, and unable to reach other minds except through the body that was made to imprison it. (W-pI.72.2:1-3)**

The body as prison is a Gnostic idea. The ego's intention for the body is as a penitentiary. The mind seems imprisoned, and this situation is extremely painful compared to the mind's freedom without having to drag around this ball and chain of clotting blood, ugly blubber, and broken bones. Even though the ego did make the body as solitary confinement, the Holy Spirit, Who is way wiser than the smart-ass ego, turns the ego's poky purpose upside out and inside down, as She tends to do, and instead uses the body for painless communication, which serves the salvation of everyone, and finally fuses into Communion. Like any other illusion the ego uses to maintain its kingdom, the Holy Spirit can reverse the ego's intended use-for-separation, and instead use-it-for-salvation. I could not write this book without a body. Jesus needed some bodies to receive ACIM. Thanks to those three: Helen, Bill, and Kenneth.

All these teachings about the body explain Jesus' teaching at the beginning of this chapter, that the healing of the body *should not be too strongly emphasized.* Yet, healing the body is not ignored either, because in this world the body can be healed, and such healing aids prayer and demonstrates the power of forgiveness. We need to remember, however, that healing of the body is only an echo or harmonic of the true healing of the mentally ill beliefs in separation, sin, guilt, fear, infirmity, and death. If the body is healed, it is a temporary side effect of true forgiveness, that permits *mind healing.*

> **The body can be healed as an effect of true forgiveness. Only that can give rememberance of immortality, which is the gift of holiness and love. Forgiveness must be given by a mind which understands that it must overlook all shadows on the holy face of Christ, among which sickness should be seen as one. Nothing but that; the sign of judgment made by brother upon brother, and the Son of God upon himself. For he has damned his body as his prison, and forgot that it is he who gave this role to it. (S-3.I.3:1-5)**

I forgot that I made the body and designed it for separation. Seemingly separate minds seem to be imprisoned within bodies. This is only illusion, not truth. The ego loves separation and whatever separates and whatever keeps us separated. The ego loves borders, barbed wire fences, and walls of defense. Ego wants walls to maintain separation. Bodies are the walls that seem to separate minds.

Healing the body is a side-effect of the pure joy I experience when I realize that all "sin" is forgiven, because it never was; sin never had reality. Sin was only a dream of sin, long gone. Gone much longer than a bad dream I had 50 years ago. Can you remember every dream you ever had? No? Why not? Dreams fade away. Eventually everyone realizes that all are truly innocent, sinless, guiltless, and fearless by the Grace of God, not ego efforts. Not only me, or her, or him, but *everyone*. When guilt is gone, sickness no longer has a defensive cause or purpose, and thus the illusion of illness disappears. Notice how often in the Gospel stories of Jesus performing miracles of physical healing He first tells the healed that her sins are forgiven. Her belief in guilt that was never real is released. This is the true healing of the cause of sickness. That a blind woman received her sight back is a temporary change. She will lose it again. She will not lose the true healing of the Atonement, true forgiveness. Even Lazarus, whom Jesus reincarnated three days after he died, had to die again.

In the above quote Jesus presents another description of sickness: a shadow *on the holy face of Christ*. He also teaches the condition of the mind that is necessary to practice forgiveness-for-salvation; it is an attitude that *demonstrates a mind which understands that it must overlook all shadows on the holy face of Christ*. Jesus here is still teaching about the cause of sickness and another definition of the cause is given. It is the same cause but expressed again in different words as He likes to do. Sickness is *the sign of judgment made by brother upon brother, and the Son of God upon himself*. The teaching about giving up judgment is also repeated. Judgment, which requires a past of separation and conflict, makes us angry, sick, and depressed. Sickness is *the sign of judgment*. Judgment is the opposite of forgiveness. Judgment is a decision against the truth. Judgment is of the mind not the body. It does not matter who I judge. Same error. In this world we will perceive shadows of suffering but Jesus asks us to *overlook all shadows* because they are lies, illusions, not real.

The mistakes I made I cannot undo alone, but with help from the Friend, the Holy Spirit, I can.

> **What he has done now must God's Son undo. But not alone. For he has thrown away the prison's key; his holy sinlessness and the remembrance of his Father's Love. Yet help is given to him in the Voice his Father placed in him. The power to heal is now his Father's gift, for through His Voice He still can reach His Son, reminding him the body may become his chosen home, but it will never be his home in truth. (S-3.I.4:1-5)**

Since I am responsible for attacking another, by judging her as guilty, I am responsible to undo this error. Since I am responsible for making the body a prison, I am responsible for choosing a different use of the body. This new choice is a choice for the Holy Spirit's use of it. The mind appears to be imprisoned in the body, and thus keeping minds separate, which is a surface illusion that I can look past. The truth is minds are joined into one shared Christ Mind. When I know this is true, I cannot be sick.

I need help to heal; I cannot do it alone, and God provides the means to help everyone: *the Voice his Father placed in him.* This is the Voice for God, the Holy Spirit, who is literally within our mind. I also need every single sister (including married ones!) because true liberation is contingent on everyone's liberation.

> **As long as a single "slave" remains to walk the earth, your release is not complete. Complete restoration of the Sonship is the only goal of the miracle-minded. (T-1.VII.3:13-14)**

If anyone is not liberated, then my *release is not complete.* I need help because I threw *away the prison's key.* Earlier Jesus used this key metaphor for teaching, which teaches that He gave us the key of forgiveness, but we do not know where the door is that the key fits. This metaphor teaches that the unhealed mind does not know what true forgiveness is. That is why we give the key to Jesus to use instead of us. This time He defines the key as *holy sinlessness and the remembrance of his Father's Love*, which is the fruit of forgiveness, already true. Yet I forgot this truth and true forgiveness reminds me. The key of sinlessness and rememberance is eternal whereas the key of forgiveness is temporary. God helps us through the Holy Spirit, Who *can still reach His Son*. That is Her job. The Holy Spirit reminds us that the body is not a true home for anyone except maybe the ego.

*   *   *

The course uses the term *memory of God* twenty times. The term above, *remembrance of his Father's Love* is similar. For a long time I did not understand this. I do not want a memory of God; I want God. A memory of anything requires the past. And the memory of anyone is not what she is. If I am craving cold cream, I want the real thing, not a memory of ice cream, right? God is not in the past. If God is gone, then a memory of Him is all I got. Jesus explains the traditional use of memory:

> **Remembering is as selective as perception, being its past tense. It is perception of the past as if it were occurring now, and still were there to see. Memory, like perception, is a skill made up by you to take the place of what God gave in your creation. (T-28.I.2:5-7)**

Memory is how we keep the past. We made memory as we made perception, as substitutes for knowledge and awareness. In our relationships we use memory to make an image of the other. This image is not who she is now. The image is cognitively constructed with the building materials of past experiences, brick by brick, stick by stick. Then I confuse the memory-made image of her, only a concept I mismade, with a sweet sister as she is now: still as God created her. Do I want a real sister or sticks and stones? My relationship ends up being with the image built on memories from the past, instead of the actual person. Remember, the special love relationship is the ego's last stand.

How is it possible that we made memory and perception? Remember the unceasing creative force of the mind. God made us like Himself. We share the Father's being and share His creative will. Yet again, with my willingness, the Holy Spirit can take anything I made for the ego's purpose and use it for God's purpose:

> **And like all the things you made, it** [memory] **can be used to serve another purpose, and to be the means for something else. It can be used to heal and not to hurt, if you so wish it be. (T-28.I.2:8-9)**

The solution to this confusion about wanting God, not the memory of God, is understanding that the Holy Spirit uses memory and remembering in a holy way and not the ego way I use it, to keep the past. The Holy Spirit uses memory to forget the past!

> **The Holy Spirit can indeed make use of memory, for God Himself is there. Yet this is not a memory of past events, but only of a present state. You are so long accustomed to believe that memory holds only what is past, that it is hard for you to realize it is a skill that can remember** *now.* **(T-28.I.4:1-3)**

The memory of God is linked to a *present state*, not the past. I need this true memory because I forgot about now. I see only the past as I remember only the past.

> **The Holy Spirit's use of memory is quite apart from time. He does not seek to use it as a means to keep the past, but rather as a way to let it go. (T-28.I.5:1-2)**

Those two verses above explain how the Holy Spirit uses memory. Memory is like the body; it is neutral. I made memory so I can keep the past, including all perceived trauma of the past that grow grievous grudges. However, I can use it instead to remember the now when I turn it over to the Holy Spirit. Sometimes a course student can go for decades without understanding a course teaching. That is a common experience of course students, including the writer. If the Teacher told the freshman that it usually takes about 25 years of study before I start to get it right, I would probably respond, "No thanks." Often, as in this case, I benefit by studying the course with an open mind. Eventually, and inevitably, the Holy Spirit clears the clouds of confusion. Now I understand how the *rememberance of his Father's love* has nothing to do with the past, and I will to remember Love's *present state*. In fact, when I remember the present, at the same time I forget the past. I cannot give attention to both at the same time. Do not most of us fear losing our memory? What if I could only remember the present? How could I make plans without memory? Oh I forgot, I don't need to make plans, or any other defenses based on the petty past, or fear of future attack.

Killing God

In the next section Jesus presents yet another definition of the cause of sickness with different words: *The cause is still the wish to die and overcome the Christ.* This is the ego's goal. Healing can be of the ego or of the Holy Spirit. Suffering of body or mind is "proof" that God is not real, or if He is real, then He doesn't care about me. Job's wife told him to curse God and die. It seems a strange desire: *to die and overcome the Christ.* Yet Jesus tells us earlier in the *Workbook: While you made plans for death, He led you gently to eternal life.* (W-pI.135.18:4) Of all the forms of defense I use to maintain my worldview and sense of separate self, *to die and overcome the Christ* was the hardest one for me to get. I did not understand this teaching for a long time (decades). Even if the teaching claimed that this anti-Christ desire to die is unconscious, why? Why would I want that?

My *wish to die and overcome the Christ* is more fully explained in *The Manual For Teachers:*

Sickness is a method, conceived in madness, for placing God's Son on his Father's throne. God is seen as outside, fierce and powerful, eager to keep all power for Himself. Only by His death can He be conquered by His Son. (M-5.I.1:7-9)

Now why would I be so opposed to God that I desire to *kill* Him? Although the prodigal son wished to separate from his father, and probably believed that his exit hurt his father, there is no mention of him wanting to kill his father. Maybe the older son wanted to kill his father after he throws a huge party for the prodigal. Sibling rivalry is separation. So is spiritual rivalry.

The above quote describes God as His Highness The Supreme Control Freak who intends to kill us all as He already did when He sent the flood, except for a few special heroes. Why would I believe God is out to get me, resulting in fear of God? Well, remember what He said to Eve first, and then Adam, after evicting us from the garden:

> *I will multiply your pains in childbearing,*
>
> *you shall give birth to your children in pain.*
>
> *Your yearning shall be for your husband,*
>
> *yet he will lord it over you.*

And then God says to Adam:

> *With suffering shall you get your food from it*
>
> *every day of your life.*
>
> *It shall yield you brambles and thistles,*
>
> *and you shall eat wild plants.*
>
> *With sweat on your brow*
>
> *shall you eat your bread,*

until you return to the soil,

as you were taken from it.

For dust you are

and to dust you shall return.

(Genesis 3:16-19. Jerusalem Bible, 1966, p.18)

If that word of god, told to Eve and Adam who represent us all, does not result in guilt and fear, then I do not know what would. Then there is the biblical story about Sodom and Gomorrah. This god of the Hebrew and Christian religions is not a nice guy. This is how we started out here. By the third chapter of Genesis, it's all over. I made a mistake that I was set up for with reverse psychology, tricked into wanting to try out duality (knowledge of good and evil, like God). It does not work and cannot work. Everything the serpent said is a lie, but we believed him. The description of suffering above, demanded by a revenge-seeking little god, is simply the fruit of duality, separation. God tells us: you are going to suffer everyday of your life until you die and return to the dust you came from. Oh my. I thought God was love. There is a reason Jesus teaches in ACIM that fear of God is the final obstacle to Peace. Given our history with this angry god, from the beginning, is it any surprise then that we desire defense from it?

How do I do that? How do I defend myself from the killer God? I must kill Him even though I cannot see Him nor know where He hides out. So, since I cannot murder him, I instead attempt to usurp his power and steal his throne. But how do I do this? Since God plans to kill me, I take His power away by killing myself before He can kill me. It's a suicide coup, my power grab. In this gnarly and gnashing game I *entirely usurp the throne:*

> **But if he chooses death himself, his weakness is his strength. Now has he given himself what God would give to him, and thus entirely usurped the throne of his Creator.** (M-5.I.2:7-8)

This is the insane defensive ego plan *to die and overcome the Christ.* If I keep this defense, then it means I do not want healing, because healing is the opposite of what I want: *to die.*

As a student of ACIM, I learn the difference between true healing and false healing, just as Jesus teaches of the distinctions between true and false forgiveness and true and false prayer.

> **Distinctions therefore must be made between true healing and its faulty counterpart. The world of opposites is healing's place, for what in Heaven could there be to heal? As prayer within the world can ask amiss and seeming charity forgive to kill, so healing can be false as well as true; a witness to the power of the world or to the everlasting Love of God. (S-3.I.5:1-3)**

Distinctions like true and false are needed in the *world of opposites,* but not in Heaven.

The above paragraph sets up the next section, *False versus True Healing.* I learn the difference between the two. Jesus reminds us again that just as there is forgiveness-to-destroy versus forgiveness-for-salvation, and ego prayers versus true prayer, there are false and true versions of healing. Healing can *witness to the power of the world or to the everlasting Love of God.*

False versus True Healing

ACIM teaches that what we experience in this world is not real; it is like a dream. The reason for this is that when the *tiny mad idea* tempted us to separate from God, we could not achieve said separation. That so-called autonomy is impossible because *ideas leave not their source.* Simply put, separation from God is impossible because it is not God's Will. Even so, I stubbornly insisted on moving out of Heaven into a place apart, like the prodigal son. God did not grant this wish and instead let Adam fall into a deep sleep and dream that he did separate from God. Then in the dream he experiences the seemingly *real effects* of that wish be his own boss, in his own high rise, in a sick virtual reality, an unbelievably tricky dream.

We learn how to avoid crashing by crashing first in the flight simulator. No matter how bad the crash, nobody gets hurt, not even the aero plane. The effects of separation are not real because the separation never happened. Yet because I believe I did crash, it seems real. The problem is a belief in the mind and hence that is where healing is. We learn what hell is like by experiencing it. Then, maybe, we won't get fooled again. That's the story in a nutshell, repeated many times in the course:

> Nothing at all has happened but that you have put yourself to sleep, and dreamed a dream in which you were an alien to yourself, and but a part of someone else's dream. The miracle does not awaken you, but merely shows you who the dreamer is. It teaches you there is a choice of dreams while you are still asleep, depending on the purpose of your dreaming. Do you wish for dreams of healing, or for dreams of death? (T-28.II.4:1-4)

And here is another version of the course metaphysics in one paragraph:

> The mind can make the belief in separation very real and very fearful, and this belief is the "devil." It is powerful, active, destructive and clearly in opposition to God, because it literally denies His Fatherhood. Look at your life and see what the devil has made. But realize that this making will surely dissolve in the light of truth, because its foundation is a lie. Your creation by God is the only Foundation that cannot be shaken, because the light is in it. Your starting point is truth, and you must return to your Beginning. Much

has been seen since then, but nothing has really happened. Your Self is still in peace, even though your mind is in conflict. You have not yet gone back far enough, and that is why you become so fearful. As you approach the Beginning, you feel the fear of the destruction of your thought system upon you as if it were the fear of death. There is no death, but there is a belief in death. (T-3.VII.5:1-11)

What is the devil? A belief in separation that seems real, frightening, powerful, active, destructive, and *clearly in opposition to God*. A mistaken mind *literally denies* God Fatherhood because it believes I made me. Hey self-made man! You really made something of yourself! Yet She gently whispers, *Be glad that something is nothing*. Move along now, nothing to see here.

Yet lies do not stand and are shadows that disappear before the Light. It is amazing how much Jesus teaches in the quote above. The teacher's digest version is one sentence: *Much has been seen since then* [the Beginning], *but nothing has really happened*. While I am still asleep I can choose what kind of dreamscape I will for. I can choose dreams of sickness and death or dreams of healing and Life. Choose Life.

Look at your life and see what the devil has made. Yipes! My life looks like a ruined mess. This looking is difficult. Pride does not want to see what the devil made. Yet without this looking, I will never be free. If instead I look at a sister and accuse her, "Look what you did. You ruined my life," then the ego rewards me with nods and applause because I have joined with the devil.

Understanding then the course's metaphysical teaching that this world and bodies are illusions, dreamed by us, and not created by God, a false healing is simply another illusion.

False healing merely makes a poor exchange of one illusion for a "nicer" one; a dream of sickness for a dream of health. This can occur at lower forms of prayer, combining with

> forgiveness kindly meant but not completely understood
> as yet. Only false healing can give way to fear, so sickness
> will be free to strike again. False healing can indeed remove
> a form of pain and sickness. But the cause remains, and
> will not lack effects. The cause is still the wish to die and
> overcome the Christ. And with this wish is death a certainty,
> for prayer is answered. (S-3.II.1:1-7)

Any form of healing may seem better than the previous illusion of sickness, but the Holy Spirit is not interested in trading one illusion for a nicer one, exchanging *a dream of sickness for a dream of health*. Both are illusions. Both dreams are destined for death. This false form of healing happens at lower rungs on the ladder of prayer, where I think I am practicing forgiveness correctly, but I do not yet understand what true forgiveness is. When a false healing is given, symptoms instead of cause are "healed." In this case, because the source of sickness is not healed, the sickness will return in another form: *sickness will be free to strike again*. The form does not matter.

False healing can heal *a form of pain and sickness*, and that makes it so tempting, yet cause remains. And cause always produces effects. There is no effect without a cause. There is also no cause without an effect. The Father is the Father because of His Daughter. If God does not have a Daughter, then He is not a Father. I am not making this up:

> Without a cause there can be no effects, and yet without
> effects there is no cause...the Father is a Father by His Son...
> Thus, the Son gives Fatherhood to his Creator...
> (T-28.II.1:1-2;4)

The Teaching About a Holy Death

From the same paragraph above in *The Song Of Prayer*, Jesus begins an important teaching about death, that lasts less than five short paragraphs. Since I plan to *die and overcome the Christ*, Jesus teaches an alternative to that ego plan:

> Yet there is a kind of seeming death that has a different
> source. It does not come because of hurtful thoughts and
> raging anger at the universe. It merely signifies the end
> has come for usefulness of body functioning. And so it is
> discarded as a choice, as one lays by a garment now outworn.
> (S-3.II.1:8-11)

This different kind of death is not death but seems like death. The body seems to die, but I am not a body, and What-I-Am cannot die, nor be attacked, nor be sick. The ego's version of a fearful death involves *hurtful thoughts and raging anger at the universe.*

The alternative to an angry death is described clearly: *It merely signifies the end has come for usefulness of body functioning.* Then Jesus uses a nice metaphor to describe this kind of death. The body is put away like worn out clothes, or clothes that no longer fit. Why would I wear jeans that are so tight they cause pain? I naturally take them off, because they hurt, just as I would quickly pull my hand off of a red-hot wood stove. I hope I am getting too big for my breeches.

Naturally, I fear death, and the older I get, the closer it seems, the larger it looms, and the quicker time passes. Death is approaching me faster and faster, as the concrete approaches after I fall off the empire state. But look how Jesus describes it:

> This is what death should be; a quiet choice, made joyfully
> and with a sense of peace, because the body has been kindly
> used to help the Son of God along the way he goes to God.
> We thank the body, then, for all the service it has given us.

> But we are thankful, too, the need is done to walk the world
> of limits, and to reach the Christ in hidden forms and clearly
> seen at most in lovely flashes. Now we can behold Him
> without blinders, in the light that we have learned to look
> upon again. (S-3.II.2:1-4)

This kind of death is joyful, peaceful, and quiet. The result of this kind of death is gratefulness and thanksgiving. I thank the body for its service and I am also grateful that *the need is done to walk the world of limits, and to reach the Christ in hidden forms and clearly seen at most in lovely flashes.* In this finite world of limits, we cannot know the infinite, and we only reach Christ in lovely, flickering flashes. Upon this kind of gentle death we receive a great blessing, to be able to behold Christ as He Is: *Now we can behold Him without blinders, in the light that we have learned to look upon again.* Hence the Heavenly song of gratefulness and thanksgiving described by Jesus from the first paragraph of *The Song Of Prayer.*

I remember a passage from the *Manual For Teachers*: where Jesus teaches that the *true conditions* of our *homecoming* are *a grateful heart and thankful mind.* And Love is not far behind:

> Remembering the name of Jesus Christ is to give thanks
> for all the gifts that God has given you. And gratitude to
> God becomes the way in which He is remembered, for love
> cannot be far behind a grateful heart and thankful mind.
> God enters easily, for these are the true conditions for your
> homecoming. (M-23.4:5-7)

Gratefulness is the heart of prayer. In prayer I thank God for forgiveness and healing and accept these graces that He already gave to all. This gratefulness grows into the Divine Love we share. This shift from ungratefulness to gratefulness is accomplished gradually by the Holy Spirit. She waits patiently for me to accept the Atonement for myself.

As I am willing to accept the truth of sinlessness and defenselessness I respond with tremendous thanksgiving. The more I experience forgiveness, the more grateful I become. Forgiven much, I thank much and love much.

Jesus continues to share a positive view of death. He calls it *liberty* and *a gentle welcome to release*. Death is not forced on me.

> We call it death, but it is liberty. It does not come in forms that seem to be thrust down in pain upon unwilling flesh, but as a gentle welcome to release. If there has been true healing, this can be the form in which death comes when it is time to rest a while from labor gladly done and gladly ended. Now we go in peace to freer air and gentler climate, where it is not hard to see the gifts we gave were saved for us. For Christ is clearer now; His vision more sustained in us; His Voice, the Word of God, more certainly our own. (S-3.II.3:1-5)

This form of a good and gentle death, however, comes with a condition. The condition is this: *if there has been true healing.* Just in case I hope that this kind of liberated death is not conditional, Jesus will repeat this teaching in the next paragraph, and repeat it again in the one after that. Remember, true healing that allows this kind of death is of the mind not the body. Jesus describes this good death in positive terms: *it is time to rest a while from labor gladly done and gladly ended.* I wonder if *to rest a while* refers to coming back again after a rest? Otherwise, this peaceful rest is eternal, and not *a while.* The beatific descriptions of this form of death go on: *Now we go in peace to freer air and gentler climate,* and, *Christ is clearer now.*

In this form of death, this *gentle passage to a higher prayer,* I let go of the *ways of earth.* The response to this kind of transition is a *grateful heart* and a *thankful mind.* In fact, this holy death can only be accepted with gratitude.

This gentle passage to a higher prayer, a kind forgiveness of
the ways of earth, can only be received with thankfulness.
Yet first true healing must have come to bless the mind with
loving pardon for the sins it dreamed about and laid upon
the world. Now are its dreams dispelled in quiet rest. Now its
forgiveness comes to heal the world and it is ready to depart
in peace, the journey over and the lessons learned.
(S-3.II.4:1-4)

But before death can happen as real blessing, *true healing must have
come to bless the mind with loving pardon for the sins it dreamed about
and laid upon the world.* The condition for this peaceful form of death
is repeated, but expanded and Jesus gives a definition of what this
true healing is: the mind is blessed with loving forgiveness for the
mistakes I thought I made, and I withdraw the judgments I projected
onto the world, and onto others. Judgment and condemnation make
the world an evil and sinful place, full of separated sinners. When
this healing happens in our seemingly defiled mind, the only place
we need healing, and the only place healing can happen, then we can
rest in peace. The nightmare of separation, sin, guilt, fear, sickness,
and death is over. When I realize true forgiveness-for-salvation, I
am *ready to depart in peace, the journey over and the lessons learned.*
What do the four it and its refer to above? Our mind.

This vision of a holy death that Jesus presents is not the version
of death that the world offers. The world's view of death is cruel and
unusual punishment, painful proof of serious sin. To the world, death
is not a blessing, but a curse, something to be avoided and feared, an
execution prepared to pay in pain the price for sin.

This is not death according to the world, for death is cruel
in its frightened eyes and takes the form of punishment for
sin. How could it be a blessing, then? And how could it be
welcome when it must be feared? What healing has occurred

in such a view of what is merely opening the gate to higher prayer and kindly justice done? Death is reward and not a punishment. But such a viewpoint must be fostered by the healing that the world cannot conceive. There is no partial healing. What but shifts illusions has done nothing. What is false cannot be partly true. If you are healed your healing is complete. Forgiveness is the only gift you give and would receive. (S-3.II.5:1-11)

If I share the world's view of death, it means that the mind seems to linger in prison, unhealed, yet. When I was depressed, I had a two-sentence, six-word philosophy: *First I suffer. Then I die.* I was not thankful or grateful. Anything good and kind that happens here is quickly taken away, a trick to tempt me to find love here where there is not even hope of finding love. The special love relationship is the ego's biggest gun. The ego pursues its goals with *fanatic insistence*:

The ego is certain that love is dangerous, and this is always its central teaching. It never puts it this way; on the contrary, everyone who believes that the ego is salvation seems to be intensely engaged in the search for love. Yet the ego, though encouraging the search for love very actively, makes one proviso; do not find it. Its dictates, then, can be summed up simply as: "Seek and do not find." This is the one promise the ego holds out to you, and the one promise it will keep. For the ego pursues its goal with fanatic insistence, and its judgment, though severely impaired, is completely consistent. (T-12.IV.1:1-6)

When I was suicidal I did not know what a holy death is: *opening the gate to higher prayer and kindly justice done.* The healed mind views death as *reward and not punishment.* Again the condition required for this form of death is given. This enlightened experience of death *must be fostered by the healing that the world cannot conceive.* That is the third time in three paragraphs that Jesus teaches the condition required for a good death. It is rare that I hear a teaching only once and get it. There is good reason why Jesus uses so much repetition. How does He describe the ego's judgment? It is *completely consistent* and *severely impaired*. It is consistent in its impairment. What is the *higher prayer*, that death opens the gate to? It is the song of thanks, Love, and union in Heaven, as described in the first introductory paragraph of *The Song Of Prayer*.

Healing is whole or it is not: *there is no partial healing*. A healing, that only replaces one illusion for another, exchanging a *dream of sickness for a dream of health*, is not the mind healing that permits a holy death: *What but shifts illusions has done nothing*. I do not receive a partial healing and I cannot accept a compromise: *What is false cannot be partially true*. If I am healed, I am healed completely, and here is the evidence of that healing: *Forgiveness is the only gift you give and would receive*. If the mind is healed, I will not judge, condemn, or attack anyone. I will not project guilt onto anyone. I will only give and accept forgiveness-for-salvation. Healing is evidence of true forgiveness, and true forgiveness is evidence of healing.

This teaching about the mind healing needed for a holy death is stated first in the *Text*. In this quote the result of this healing is described as *revelation with lasting effect*:

Only the healed mind can experience revelation with lasting effect, because revelation is an experience of pure joy.
(T-5.I.1:3)

In order to experience *pure joy*, this mind healing is needed. Pure joy is the state of a healed mind. A holy death is not the only benefit. We cannot experience pure joy and guilt at the same time. They are not compatible.

I love how consistent the course is. Here is more confirmation regarding sickness, death, and responsibility for the cruel choices I made, from Lesson 152:

No one can suffer loss unless it be his own decision. No one
suffers pain except his choice elects this state for him. No
one can grieve nor fear nor think him sick unless these are
the outcomes that he wants. And no one dies without his
own consent. Nothing occurs but represents your wish, and
nothing is omitted that you choose. (W-pI.152.1:1-5)

No one dies without his own consent. I may not remember this consent
just as I do not remember making a decision to be sick.

The last sentence of this section (below) is a joyful statement
describing the liberation and reward that death allows the truly healed
mind: *At last the gate of Heaven opens and God's Son is free to enter in
the home that stands ready to welcome him, and was prepared before
time was and still but waits for him.* (S-3.II.6:4) A home was prepared
for us before time happened, and still waits for us. That gives true
hope. I may seem houseless now but I am hoping for that home.

There is one more paragraph in this section that returns to the
teaching on discernment between false and true healing. False healing focuses on the body only and does not heal the cause of sickness
that is in the mind, not the body:

False healing rests upon the body's cure, leaving the cause of
illness still unchanged, ready to strike again until it brings
a cruel death in seeming victory. It can be held at bay a little
while, and there can be brief respite as it waits to take its
vengeance on the Son of God. Yet it cannot be overcome
until all faith in it has been laid by, and placed upon God's
substitute for evil dreams; a world in which there is no veil of
sin to keep it dark and comfortless. At last the gate of Heaven
opens and God's Son is free to enter in the home that stands
ready to welcome him, and was prepared before time was and
still but waits for him. (S-3.II.6:1-4)

A healing that correctly focuses on the mind may lead to a physical healing, but that is not its true intention. Jesus says the body may follow in healing, or not. On the third page of the *Text*, He first presents this teaching in the 35th miracle principal: *Miracles are expressions of love, but they may not always have observable effects.* (T-1.I.35:1) Observable effects refer to the body. If the mind is healed, I do not observe it like I do the body. Mind is not visible, but it is knowable.

It is not the true healer's intention to heal the body. If that is my intention, then I am an unhealed healer and make the mistake of praying for the echo, the overtones of the true healing, instead of the true song of healing. It is important to understand the difference. It is easy to be impressed with acts of bodily healing but is it a miracle, or magic? False healing, that does not heal cause, is always temporary. Even in true healing of the cause, if the body follows, that bodily healing is temporary, though the mind healing is complete and permanent.

Faith in false healing must be exchanged for God's solution to the nightmare detour into fear: a forgiven world, viewed through the understanding vision of Christ: *a world in which there is no veil of sin to keep it dark and comfortless.*

This concludes the second section of the chapter on healing, about learning the difference between true and false healing, and the blessed teaching about dying a holy death. The teaching about death occurs in the chapter on healing because of the prerequisite for a holy death: the true healing of the mind.

Separation versus Union and Exclusion versus Inclusion

The third section in the chapter on healing starts with further identification of false healing. Any healing that does not heal the cause of sickness (separation from God and each other), fails to heal truly. If the body seems healed yet the mind is not healed, healing is not whole; it is partial: *Therefore it still deceives.*

False healing heals the body in a part, but never as a whole. Its separate goals become quite clear in this, for it has not removed the curse of sin that lies on it. Therefore it still deceives. Nor is it made by one who understands the other is exactly like himself. For it is this that makes true healing possible. When false, there is some power that another has, not equally bestowed on both as one. Here is the separation shown. And here the meaning of true healing has been lost, and idols have arisen to obscure the unity that is the Son of God. (S-3.III.1:1-8)

If the body is "healed" but *the curse of sin is not removed*, healing is false. True healing, the effect of true forgiveness, removes the curse of sin, which removes guilt, which removes the fear that blocks the awareness of Love. This teaching is also stated in the *Workbook*:

Atonement does not heal the sick, for that is not a cure. It takes away the guilt that makes the sickness possible. And that is cure indeed. For sickness now is gone, with nothing left to which it can return. (W-pI.140.4:4-7)

I appreciate how consistent the *Text*, *Workbook*, and *Manual For Teachers* are with *The Song Of Prayer*.

In order for sickness to return, it needs something called guilt to return to. If the guilt is gone, sickness cannot return. True healing heals both guilt and sickness because one causes the other in a vicious circle. Guilt causes sickness and then sickness is cause of more guilt and more guilt produces more sickness, and so on as guilt and illness inflate to suicidal proportions. Remove the cause and the effect collapses with no support. (M-3.II.3:11)

Jesus presents another example of false healing and this discussion is important enough to last three paragraphs in this short pamphlet. This idea also reinforces a fundamental and primary teaching in ACIM: a radical inclusion, and the parity of us all as one. In three words: *Everyone is included.* I like how Robert Hunter put it in his lyric: *Everyone's playing in the heart of gold band.* There are no differences between us. Sure, I perceive plenty of disparities if I identify as a separate individual, but that identity is a passing illusion and my deceptive perception is projection. To know that there is no difference between a sister and myself is not seen with eyeballs but understood and known as I think with Christ.

When it comes to healing, if I consider myself to be different from a sister, then true healing is impossible. False healing is partial and not *made by one who understands the other is exactly like himself,* and thus it is the recognition that a sister is exactly like me *that makes true healing possible.* In fact, realizing this radically inclusive quality of the Atonement is the goal of the miracle which saves us the thousands of years it takes to learn of this equal opportunity otherwise, without the miracle. The opportunity is the option for unity: oppt-for-unity.

This true idea of complete parity is not congruent with Christianity where Jesus is seen as different from us, and we are seen as different from each other. There are the sheep and the goats. Of eight billion bodies 144,000 make it. How many of us don't make it? About 7,000,856,000, the ego's odds. There are the few, the chosen elite elect, and then there are the many, going to hell in a hurry. In ACIM Jesus is our elder brother, the exact same as we are except for one difference that is temporary. The only difference is that He is the first to complete His part in the Atonement. And because of this, He is in charge of the Atonement, a temporary position, until the Atonement is completed. ACIM describes this completion as the *complete restoration of the Sonship.* (T.1.VII.3:14) Thus, the only difference between Jesus and us is time, and time is a temporary illusion. We help complete the Atonement by following Him, our elder brother. We are not to worship Him. Awe is reserved only for the Creator of Perfection, not the perfectly created. (T-1.II.3:3)

Jesus does not want a separating power differential between Him and us. If fact, it is the opposite. He is ending the separation, not promoting it. If I feel I am unworthy of Jesus, or different from Him, then I am rejecting Him and His teaching, for such is not the Truth. The Truth is this: minds that seem separate are *already* joined with the mind of Jesus into the Christ Mind, the one Child of God. All minds joined together is the Christ Mind. What may seem like differences between us are illusionary because these differences are temporary as time, part of the dream. Time is an illusion. It seems real to us only because we believe it is true.

Here is another passage where Jesus refers back to His life on earth and He uses a new term to describe the Holy Spirit and again stresses inclusion:

> **As a man and also one of God's creations, my right thinking, which came from the Holy Spirit or the Universal Inspiration, taught me first and foremost that this Inspiration is for all. I could not have It myself without knowing this. (T-5.I.4:6-7)**

The idea of a radical, total, and inclusive equality is a main course theme. This unconditional inclusion does not include egos or bodies because they are not real and were not created by God. This ACIM teaching is not compatible with Christian theology, with its doctrine on resurrection of the body, and the emphasis on flesh. *The Word was made flesh.* Not only that, but we are encouraged to literally eat His flesh and drink His blood. It is not a metaphor.

In the above quote from the *Text*, the Holy Spirit is referred to as the *Universal Inspiration.* Although there is much repetition in the course, that term is never repeated. What did Jesus learn *first and foremost* about this Inspiration? He learned that this *Universal Inspiration is for all*, and I cannot participate in it if I exclude anyone. If I exclude anyone, I automatically exclude myself. Jesus Himself *could not have It without knowing this.* I know Christians who believe that Jesus is exclusive. Yet His inclusiveness is taught in the New Testament as well. Remember the story about the Good Shepherd who leaves the 99 sheep to go find the one percent lost lamb? 99% is not whole. 99.99% is not whole. 100% is whole. This is the good news. Why would I want bad news instead? I am sorry sinner, but you are going to hell, and before that permanent pain, you are going to suffer every day and for all eternity. Why this Christian dichotomy? Because some sinners are forgiven and most are not. How could that be? Because the ego teaches us that Christ is exclusive to the vast majority of us.

What may be difficult to understand is that the ego is not saved and if I identify as a body/ego I can wrongly think that this concept of self is saved, because I mis-identify it as me. A similar mistake is to try to reform the ego, resist it, convert it, change it into a good and loving ego, etc. If the ego is to be saved it must first repent of the bad ego and change into a kind ego. Not going to happen! It is also a mistake to try to kill the ego. If I want to kill the ego I make the mental error of assuming that the ego is real. The ego is not killed, nor promoted, nor included; it is relinquished as unreal. The ego is the vine-disconnected branch that cannot produce real grapes for the good wine because it does not, cannot, and will not, abide in Christ. Remember, the ego wants *to overcome the Christ*. Ego is made by us by miscreating it. Since it is not real, it is not saved. Because there is no separation in Heaven, ego cannot participate in *The Song Of Prayer*. Sorry old buddy, I don't mean to be mean but you do.

In the next paragraph, Jesus continues to teach about the importance of equality and inclusion. If I see any healer, including doctors, as different from me, then healing becomes *healing-to-separate*.

> Healing-to-separate may seem to be a strange idea. And
> yet it can be said of any form of healing that is based on
> inequality of any kind. These forms may heal the body, and
> indeed are generally limited to this. Someone knows better,
> has been better trained, or is perhaps more talented and wise.
> Therefore, he can give healing to the one who stands beneath
> him in his patronage. The healing of the body can be done

by this because, in dreams, equality cannot be permanent. The shifts and change are what the dream is made of. To be healed appears to be to find a wiser one who, by his arts and learning, will succeed. (S-3.III.2:1-8)

In the dream world bodies can be healed by medical procedures, but the inequality of doctor and patient remains because *in dreams, equality cannot be permanent.*

In this world, there is not equality, except perhaps a temporary one. One of the qualities of this dualistic dream world is constant shifting and changing: *The shifts and change are what the dream is made of.* Why is impermanence a good thing? It is positive because it means illusions are temporary, including the illusion of an identity as a separate individual. Not only do illusions not last, but they are not even real in the first place. Impermanence proves that illusions are not true just because they fade away. God, Heaven, Truth, Christ, Holy Spirit, Joy, Peace, and Prayer are symbols for the eternal, or non-temporal and non-dual Truth that includes unspeakable Love and Knowledge.

Again, Jesus emphasizes equality, which is not the way of the world. In the world's eyes, a doctor is seen as more important and she is paid sizable sums for a single surgery, emphasizing the disparity, unless she is a doctor without borders. Jesus is firm in this: *True healing cannot come from inequality assumed and then accepted as the truth.*

Someone knows better; this the magic phrase by which the body seems to be the aim of healing as the world conceives of it. And to this wiser one another goes to profit by his learning and his skill; to find in him the remedy for pain. How can that be? True healing cannot come from inequality assumed and then accepted as the truth, and used to help restore the wounded and to calm the mind that suffers from the agony of doubt. (S-3.III.3:1-4)

Is it not apparent how in this world there is disparity between the healer (someone who knows better) and the sick, who willingly pay doctors and therapists even though any "cure" is temporary? Every patient ever treated by a professional healer has died or will die. Every doctor or psychologist dies as well. Any and all physical healing is temporary. Welcome to the world.

After studying all these teachings about what healing is and what it isn't, I might assume that any attempt to aid the dream body is a mistake, substituting a dream of health for a dream of sickness. Jesus addresses this question next:

> **Is there a role for healing, then, that one can use to offer help for someone else? In arrogance the answer must be "no." But in humility there is indeed a place for helpers. It is like the role that helps in prayer, and lets forgiveness be what it is meant to be. You do not make yourself the bearer of the special gift that brings the healing. You but recognize your oneness with the one who calls for help. For in this oneness is his separate sense dispelled, and it is this that made him sick. There is no point in giving remedy apart from where the source of sickness is, for never thus can it be truly healed. (S-3.III.4:1-8)**

Jesus asks, should anyone help another to heal? If I think the answer is "no," then that answer is arrogant. In the first chapter of *The Song Of Prayer*, He teaches that humility is the fruit of prayer. Healers are humble holy helpers. If am to be this kind of helper/healer/teacher, I do so as an equal to everyone, not as someone different from them whom God blessed with special healing powers: *You do not make yourself the bearer of the special gift that brings the healing.* If I do that, then I am performing healing-to-separate, because I have this special gift, and you do not. In other words, we are different and therefore separate. I do not heal but I allow Jesus, or the Holy Spirit, to facilitate healing through me. I am not the author of healing. He will give us more details as to how healing happens.

The key to performing true healing is to recognize the oneness, equality, and unity of everyone, without exception. Helping healers are interested in the complete restoration of the Children of God as the one, inclusive Child of God: *You but recognize your oneness with the one who calls for help.* Why is this recognition so important? Remember that the cause of sickness is separation and its fruits. When I will to join with a sister, I am removing the false claim of separation: *For in this oneness is his separate sense dispelled, and it is this that made him sick.* The last sentence in the above quote repeats again the fundamental idea that any healing that does not heal the cause of suffering is incomplete, and there is no point to even attempting healing-to-separate.

These ideas about realizing equality and oneness in order to heal and be healed are first mentioned in the *Text*:

Healing is a thought by which two minds perceive their oneness and become glad. (T-5.I.1:1)

What becomes glad? Minds that perceive oneness. What is healing? A thought, a simple change of mind. The end game: lots of framented minds integrate and transform into one Big Mind, the Christ Mind, that is no longer wrong-minded nor right-minded but one-minded.

How lovely does the world become in just that single instant when you see the truth about yourself reflected there. Now you are sinless and behold your sinlessness. Now you are holy and perceive it so. And now the mind returns to its Creator; the joining of the Father and the Son, the Unity of unities that stands behind all joining but beyond them all. God is not seen but only understood. His Son is not attacked but recognized. (C-4.8:1-6)

After all the separated minds of God rejoin into the Christ Mind, the Father and His Child are reunited as One. This is the grandest of all reunions. In the course, this ultimate re-joining is called the *Unity of unities.* Love and unity go together because love draws us into union.

Below Jesus offers an interesting take on His Gospel teaching to love my neighbor as myself as He teaches us the *healer's prayer*:

> **It is impossible for a child of God to love his neighbor except as himself. That is why the healer's prayer is:**
>
> *Let me know this brother as I know myself.* (T-5.in.3:6-8)

The *only way* I can love my neighbor is as myself. The word let indicates this is a prayer, even though it is not formally addressed to God. The prayer could be prayed, *Dear God, let me know this sister as I know myself. Dear Lord, let me love this sister as I love myself.* Why as myself? Because God has one Child. In other words, Sisters-Я-Us.

True healers understand that we are all one with our Source and with each other: our Identity is as the Christ, the one Child of God, and thus giving Fatherhood to God. Why does Jesus speak of Sons below rather than the singular Son? Because here He is speaking of healers, and thus must be referring to duality where healing is possible. There is no healing, nor healers, in Heaven.

> **Healers there are, for they are Sons of God who recognize their Source, and understand that all their Source creates is one with them. This is the remedy that brings relief which cannot fail. It will remain to bless for all eternity. It heals no part, but wholly and forever. Now the cause of every malady has been revealed exactly as it is. And in that place is written now the holy Word of God. Sickness and separation must be healed by love and union. Nothing else can heal as God established healing. Without Him there is no healing, for there is no love.** (S-3.III.5:1-9)

The sick do not remember their Identity as One, and the healer helps to heal by reminding them of their truth and Who made Whom. Freed of separation we are freed of sickness. What is *the remedy that brings relief which cannot fail?* Recognizing our Source and our oneness with everything our Source creates. Our wholeness as oneness is inclusive because if one part is missing, we are not whole. The Unity of unities *will remain to bless for all eternity.*

Partial healing, although tempting, is not true healing. This is true healing: *It heals no part, but wholly and forever.* The cause of any kind of suffering: physical, mental, emotional, or spiritual, is revealed exactly as it is: separation and its effects: sin, guilt, fear, sickness, conflict, attack, defensiveness, death, and hell. In healing I am making an exchange. I exchange the dream of separation for the Truth of joining: *And in that place is written now the holy Word of God.* This exchange is described in many ways in the course: separation for joining, wrong-mindedness for right-mindedness, judgment for forgiveness, specialness for sameness, special relationship for holy relationship.

At the end of the paragraph above, Jesus adds another factor into healing: Love: *Sickness and separation must be healed by love and union.* Early in this book, we looked at the relationship between Love and prayer and now it resurfaces: miracles are maximal expressions of Love. Love draws together: joining creates Union while fear, based on guilt, based on sin, and based on separation, separates. Love draws us to Itself, yet we avoid what we fear. If someone is bullying me at school, do I choose to sit next to her at lunch? No, I sit as far away as possible, unless I am a bigger bully. Love is necessary for healing, as *God established healing,* because *Without Him there is no healing, for there is no love.* No God means no Love because God Is Love. Healing comes from God's Love, not human love. God uses His teachers and healers as channels for His Love, peace, healing, and joy, if there is willingness, if we truly desire it, through the Holy Spirit, as Saint Francis prayed: *Make me a channel of Your Peace.* The desire for it is prayer of the heart.

The Holy Spirit guides us in healing. For this to happen, we learn how to listen to Her, and this receptive listening is prayer. If I learn how to listen, I *will never fail to bring His kindly remedy to those He sends* to me.

> God's Voice alone can tell you how to heal. Listen, and you will never fail to bring His kindly remedy to those He sends to you, to let Him heal them, and to bless all those who serve with Him in healing's name. The body's healing will occur because its cause has gone. And now without a cause, it cannot come again in different form. Nor will death any more be feared because it has been understood. There is no fear in one who has been truly healed, for love has entered now where idols used to stand, and fear has given way at last to God. (S-3.III.6:1-6)

The Holy Spirit sends people to me for healing but the true healer is God, through the Holy Spirit, through me. If I am willing to listen to the Holy Spirit and serve as a holy helper in healing, then the Holy Spirit will never fail *to bless all those who serve with Him in healing's name.*

By now, I might be used to Jesus' use of repetition. Because I am so conditioned with wrong-minded, egotistical thinking, it takes many reminders before I start to get it right. The body's healing may happen if the cause of sickness, which is in the mind and not the body, is healed: *The body's healing will occur because its cause has gone.* I leave the effect of the echoes and overtones of healing to God. When true healing heals the cause (guilt in the mind), there can no longer be effects. Effects require a cause. A false healing may heal the body temporarily, but because the mind is not healed, cause, and effects, will continue. The form of the effects may change, but the form does not matter. The only solution is to heal the cause, and then effects heal as an echo of the true healing that is within mind. The cause is only a belief, not a body-belief but a mind-belief.

The teaching about death is repeated in one sentence: *Nor will death any more be feared because it has been understood.* If the mind is healed with forgiveness, Love, and Union, then the block to the awareness of Love, that is fear, caused by the claim of guilt over the separation, disappears, and no longer fearing death, nor fearing my Father, I can receive and accept a holy death. There can be no fear remaining when Love blesses us with Union. In the unitive state, Love replaces fear: *There is no fear in one who has been truly healed, for love has entered now where idols used to stand, and fear has given way at last to God.*

This ends the third section, *Separation versus Healing*, and we move on to the fourth and final section, *The Holiness of Healing*, which ends the chapter on Healing and also ends *The Song Of Prayer.*

The Holiness of Healing

True healers are holy because they share the *thought of God.* Love, healing, and peace are holy. Healers are described as t*he Holy Spirit's voice, through whom He speaks for God, Whose Voice He is.* When I first read *the Holy Spirit's voice,* I thought that the word *voice* being lowercase was a typo, because it is usually uppercase as it is in the same sentence: *Whose Voice He is.* Uppercase Voice refers to the Voice for God, the Holy Spirit. Lowercase voice refers to the many voices in duality. In this case, voice refers to human healers who become the voice for the Holy Spirit. The Holy Spirit can speak for God through us. When Jesus was on earth, He was the manifestation of the Holy Spirit. Now He invites you and I to be the manifestation of the Holy Spirit.

> **How holy are the healed! For in their sight their brothers share their healing and their love. Bringers of peace,–the Holy Spirit's voice, through whom He speaks for God, Whose Voice He is,–such are God's healers. They but speak for Him and never for themselves. They have no gifts but those they**

have from God. And these they share because they know
that this is what He wills. They are not special. They are holy.
They have chosen holiness, and given up all separate dreams
of special attributes through which they can bestow unequal
gifts on those less fortunate. Their healing has restored their
wholeness so they can forgive, and join the song of prayer in
which the healed sing of their union and their thanks to God.
(S-3.IV.1:1-10)

A humble holy healer gives all the credit to God and does not let miracles or healing go to her head, as if she is the special healer: *They but
speak for Him and never for themselves. They have no gifts but those
they have from God.*

One of the important teachings of ACIM is that giving and
receiving are the same. I receive whatever I give. I am healed as I
let the Holy Spirit heal through me: *Their healing has restored their
wholeness so they can forgive.* The implication in this teaching is that
I must be healed and whole in order to truly forgive. When healing
restores wholeness, I can forgive. Perhaps this is why Jesus teaches
that I don't understand forgiveness. I need to be healed whole before
I can understand true forgiveness. I share the gifts God gives me. In
this way God's gifts increase. If I give someone an idea, I do not lose
the idea. It is not like money. I keep the idea and it grows greater as we
share it. This is the economy of Heaven. All true ideas only increase.

God, Who encompasses all being, created beings who have
everything individually, but who want to share it to increase
their joy. Nothing real can be increased except by sharing.
That is why God created you. Divine Abstraction takes joy in
sharing. (T-4.VII.5:1-4)

We share forgiveness, prayer, and healing because it is God's Will,
which we share with Him: *And these they share because they know
that this is what He wills.*

Early in the *Text* Jesus teaches the proper thoughts and attitude for healing both myself and everyone:

You can do much on behalf of your own healing and that of others if, in a situation calling for help, you think of it this way:

> *I am here only to be truly helpful.*
>
> *I am here to represent Him Who sent me.*
>
> *I do not have to worry about what to say or what to do, because He Who sent me will direct me.*
>
> *I am content to be wherever He wishes, knowing He goes there with me.*
>
> *I will be healed as I let Him teach me to heal.*

(T-2.V.A.18.8:1-6)

This faithful attitude is a result of developing trust in God.

Holy healers make the choice for God by choosing to join with Jesus or the Holy Spirit instead of joining with the ego: *They are not special. They are holy. They have chosen holiness.* Joining with ego or joining with the Holy Spirit are both choices; I cannot have both any more than I can have death and life at the same time. With the help of the Holy Spirit true healers learn and understand the difference between healing-to-separate and healing-for-salvation, and they give up investment in the dream. They give up *all separate dreams of special attributes through which they can bestow unequal gifts on those less fortunate.* If I think I have special healing powers, and that in a spectacle of magnificent generosity I bestow gifts of healing on a sick sister, then I am practicing healing-to-separate. The last sentence of the paragraph above refers back to the first paragraph in *The Song Of Prayer*, where the true form of prayer, as it is in Heaven, is described again: *and join the song of prayer in which the healed sing of their union and their thanks to God.* The qualities of this prayer are Love, Union, and Thanksgiving. Who joins in this Song? The *healed*.

Healing is the witness that forgiveness is true. Without forgiveness, separation remains and healing is blocked, because separation causes sickness. Healing is also an aid to prayer because without healing, I do not know what true forgiveness is, and without true forgiveness, its Sister, prayer, loses her wings, and cannot rise above the lowest rung of the ladder. Healing is also a blessing of mercy: *the effect of mercy truly taught.* Hence, I learn of the mutual co-dependence of healing, forgiveness, and prayer.

> As witness to forgiveness, aid to prayer, and the effect of mercy truly taught, healing is blessing. And the world responds in quickened chorus through the voice of prayer. Forgiveness shines its merciful reprieve upon each blade of grass and feathered wing and all the living things upon the earth. Fear has no haven here, for love has come in all its holy oneness. Time remains only to let the last embrace of prayer rest on the earth an instant, as the world is shined away. This instant is the goal of all true healers, whom the Christ has taught to see His likeness and to teach like Him. (S-3.IV.2:1-6)

Jesus describes the final period before time ends: *Time remains only to let the last embrace of prayer rest on the earth an instant, as the world is shined away.* I kind of like the idea of the world being *shined away.* Shine away you crazy dream diamond.

Whom has Christ taught to see His likeness and to teach like Him? True healers. At this final stage, Love replaces fear: *Fear has no haven here, for love has come in all its holy oneness.* The holy instant of liberation, when the world is shined away, is the goal of all healers: *This instant is the goal of all true healers.* At this point, forgiveness and healing have completed their service, and are shined away with joy and thanksgiving that God gave us these means, along with the greatest gift and help, prayer, or Holy Communion, that shines on forever. The journey without distance is completed because we have learned from the Christ how to see His Face in all life, and how to Love as He Loves. We are ones *whom the Christ has taught to see His likeness and to teach like Him.*

Honestly, I am not sure how to interpret this line from the above quote: *Forgiveness shines its merciful reprieve upon each blade of grass and feathered wing and all the living things upon the earth.* I might interpret it as metaphor, but it seems a strange metaphor to use in the same paragraph that speaks of shining away the world. What if the merciful reprieve of forgiveness does shine on *all the living things upon the earth*? Does that include the mosquito I just swatted, and the crazy alligator that wants some flesh for lunch? Are the living things on earth shined away with the world? How many blades of grass are there? How many plants, birds, fish, insects, animals, and amebae are there? There are more than 50,000 different species of beetles alone on the earth. Yet despite the abundance of life forms on earth, it is a bloody violent place. To eat, or to be eaten, that is the question.

> **And so do all things live because of death. Devouring is nature's "law of life." God is insane, and fear alone is real.** (M-27.3:6-8)

Did God design the eat or be eaten policy? If He did then God is insane.

That quote above about *all the living things* sounds similar to something Pierre Teilhard de Chardin (1881-1955) might say. And it reminds me of St. Paul's teaching that all of creation is groaning and waiting for liberation, which Teilhard de Chardin called the Omega Point. He was a Jesuit paleontologist and a mystic and believed that the physical world is evolving into a spiritual state. Five days before he died Teilhard de Chardin said that he hoped he would die on an Easter Sunday. Five days later, on Easter Sunday 1955, he had a heart attack and died suddenly. Seems like a holy death to me. For myself, I don't know if Teilhard de Chardin's theology is true or not. I am okay with not knowing; I don't need to know that now, and I guess I'll find out soon enough. His ideas were censured by the Catholic Church, as were the ideas of St. John of the Cross (who was actually put in prison), and as were the ideas of Thomas Merton, late in his life. For Merton, that a U.S. cardinal declared the Vietnam War a "just war," just about drove Fr. Louis insane. Using a condom is sin for a married couple but dropping napalm on women and children is just fine.

Jesus asks us to think about how holy it is to help Him heal. Is there a holier way to be? Why is true healing so holy? Because the Cause of it is God.

> **Think what it means to help the Christ to heal! Can anything be holier than this? God thanks His healers, for He knows the Cause of healing is Himself, His Love, His Son, restored as His completion and returned to share with Him creation's holy joy. Do not ask partial healing, nor accept an idol for rememberance of Him Whose Love has never changed and never will. You are as dear to Him as is the whole of His creation, for it lies in you as His eternal gift. What need have you for shifting dreams within a sorry world? Do not forget the gratitude of God. Do not forget the holy grace of prayer. Do not forget forgiveness of God's Son. (S-3.IV.3:1-9)**

God thanks His healers, for He knows the Cause of healing is Himself, His Love, His Son, restored as His completion and returned to share with Him creation's holy joy. Who writes sentences like that? That single sentence could be unpacked into a whole book. God is grateful for His holy helpers. Then a quick sentence reminding us not to fall away from the truth: *Do not ask partial healing, nor accept an idol for rememberance of Him Whose Love has never changed and never will.* What is a partial healing? A partial healing is an attempt to heal the body without healing the mind. Healing is also partial if it is not radically inclusive. Healing is the inheritance of *everyone*, without exception. What is an idol? Anything that appears outside of me. Healing could become an idol if I am not careful.

Next Jesus expresses the Father's gentle Love for me: *You are as dear to Him as is the whole of His creation, for it lies in you as His eternal gift.* If I understand this correctly, Jesus is saying that the whole of God's creation is within us and given to us as His Eternal Gift. Divine Abstraction is a Sharer by nature. Do I prefer this sorry dream world to His Gift of Everything? *What need have you for shifting dreams within a sorry world?* The last three lines in this paragraph I like to view in verse rather than prose:

Do not forget the gratitude of God.

Do not forget the holy grace of prayer.

Do not forget forgiveness of God's Son.

Prayer is a holy gift. Jesus reminds us not to forget three things: *the gratitude of God, the holy grace of prayer, and the forgiveness of God's Son.* The strange truth is I tend to forget, so He repeats reminders. The combination of true forgiveness and true prayer leads to the mind healing that we thank God for. Forgetting is a sign of resistance to the Truth of Identity that ends ego. I will to forget the ego's thought system instead.

> **Learning is impossible without memory since it must be consistent to be remembered. That is why the Holy Spirit's teaching is a lesson in remembering. I said before that He teaches remembering and forgetting, but the forgetting is only to make the remembering consistent. You forget in order to remember better. (T-7.II.6:2-5)**

Every time the Holy Spirit helps me to re-remember, resistance by forgetting decreases. When the ego rears its killing thoughts, forget about it and do not forget to laugh. I'm sorry ego, I forgot your name.

The next paragraph starts with a formula. First, I forgive, because without forgiveness, the wings of prayer are clipped, and prayer cannot rise up to the Father. Then, with a forgiven and forgiving heart, I pray for true healing.

> **You first forgive, then pray, and you are healed. Your prayer has risen up and called to God, Who hears and answers. You have understood that you forgive and pray but for yourself. And in this understanding you are healed. In prayer you have united with your Source, and understood that you have never left. This level cannot be attained until there is no hatred in your heart, and no desire to attack the Son of God.**
> **(S-3.IV.4:1-6)**

With forgiveness, prayer soars like a pair of hawks who do not flap their wings going nowhere as chickens and quail do: *Your prayer has risen up and called to God, Who hears and answers.* Hawks seem to rise and hover high in the sky without effort. Without the weight of guilt, heavy as hell, I can fly free. I want to pray like that. If I get the first two parts of the recipe right, I heal and I am healed. This is the not-so-secret formula: *You first forgive, then pray, and you are healed.* Jesus then repeats the earlier teaching: *You have understood that you forgive and pray but for yourself. And in this understanding you are healed.* Except now He refers to this understanding not as something I need to learn, but as something I have learned: *You have understood.* This learning leads to understanding, which is the corrected perception. What is understood? I understand that I only forgive, pray for, and heal My Self because there is only one of us here.

Also in the above quote, Jesus describes a unitive form of prayer that not all can reach yet, and He teaches us the condition for this level of prayer: *In prayer you have united with your Source, and understood that you have never left. This level cannot be attained until there is no hatred in your heart, and no desire to attack the Son of God.* Prayer that unites us with our Source is unitive prayer, where we rest in God. Prayer does not create a new union; it reveals the union already and always present, now. The condition for this level of prayer: a pure heart. All hatred, judgment, condemnation, and attack are undone as unreal and now I am ready for Heaven.

Who Heals Whom?

Although healers help facilitate healing, healing does not come from them. Healing comes from within the patient's own mind:

> **The light of Christ in him is his release, and it is this that answers to his call. (S-2.III.5:4)**

Just as I do not choose the form of forgiveness, I do not choose the form of healing.

As a healed-healer it is not the laying on of hands, or words she might say that help healing. It is simply the healer's presence, in her right mind, that reminds the patient of her own truth about her own Identity, and eventually remember her own decision for sickness that she can now reverse. The Holy Spirit is already in the patient's mind, but she is unaware of that, as she is unaware that she decided to be sick, and as she is unaware of her true Identity, which cannot be sick.

> **A patient decides that this is so, and he recovers. If he decides against recovery, he will not be healed. Who is the physician? Only the mind of the patient himself. The outcome is what he decides that it is. (M-5.II.2:3-7)**

What does the patient decide? The patient learns that sickness is a decision that she can re-verse, and will reverse, when she understands why she chose sickness, the purpose it had in her own plan to defend herself. She learns that sickness is of the mind, not the body. Seeing the insanity and the fruit of her own plan makes reversing her decision easier and logical.

> **What do guilt and sickness, pain, disaster and all suffering mean now? Having no purpose, they are gone. And with them also go all the effects they seemed to cause. (M-5.II.4:7-9)**

When she realizes that suffering is not serving any true purpose, she lets it go. Yet without that suffering in the first place she would not suspect anything was wrong.

> How could this readiness be reached save through the sight of all your misery, and the awareness that your plan has failed, and will forever fail to bring you peace and joy of any kind? Through this despair you travel now, yet it is but illusion of despair. (T-24.II.14:2-3)

What readiness is Jesus teaching about? The readiness to accept the Atonement for myself; the readiness to exchange the ego's plan for salvation for the Holy Spirit's; the readiness to accept the healing already received. Only in the miserable awareness that the plan I made failed and will continue to fail will I be convinced to seek a better way.

Therefore, since healing comes from her own mind, as did sickness, her healing amounts to a change of mind. The healer cannot bring about this change of mind for the patient but the healer can demonstrate this change of mind in her own life.

> If the patient must change his mind in order to be healed, what does the teacher of God do? Can he change the patient's mind for him? Certainly not. (M-5.III.1:1-3)

So what does the healer or teacher of God do? She reminds the sick of the truth through her presence and *thoughts*.

> To them [the sick] God's teachers come, to represent another choice which they had forgotten. The simple presence of a teacher of God is a reminder. His thoughts ask for the right to question what the patient has accepted as true. (M-5.III.2:1-3)

The healed healer helps by representing what a healed mind is and her *simple presence* reminds the patient of the truth. The healer's thoughts ask permission to question the patient's assumptions.

With God's Word in their minds they come in benediction,
not to heal the sick but to remind them of the remedy God
has already given them. It is not their hands that heal. It is
not their voice that speaks the Word of God. They merely
give what has been given them. Very gently they call to their
brothers to turn away from death: "Behold, you Son of God,
what life can offer you. Would you choose sickness in place of
this?" (M-5.III.2:7-12)

How do I call a sister to turn from death to life? *Very gently.*

Not once do the advanced teachers of God consider the
forms of sickness in which their brother believes. To do
this is to forget that all of them have the same purpose, and
therefore are not really different. They seek for God's Voice
in this brother who would so deceive himself as to believe
God's Son can suffer. And they remind him that he did not
make himself, and must remain as God created him. They
recognize illusions can have no effect. The truth in their
minds reaches out to the truth in the minds of their brothers,
so that illusions are not reinforced. They are thus brought
to truth; truth is not brought to them. So are they [illusions]
dispelled, not by the will of another, but by the union of
the one Will with itself. And this is the function of God's
teachers; to see no will as separate from their own, nor theirs
as separate from God's. (M-5.III.3:1-9)

The true healer reminds the patient of their shared Identity, which
is Christ.

Although there are many forms of sickness, the form does not
matter because they all serve the same purpose. True healing is concerned with uncovering the single purpose of sickness, as a defense
mechanism, regardless of the form of sickness. Many forms, one
purpose. The healer seeks for the Holy Spirit, already in the patient's

mind, and reminds the patient about the Truth: You did not create yourself and thus you remain as God created you, perfect and sinless. This is communicated to the mind, not the body's ears. The truth in the healer's mind reaches out to the truth in her sister's mind that is temporarily confused about her identity by believing illusions. This is what true psychotherapy is.

The last two sentences in the quote above teach that the illusions causing sickness are not dispelled by the healer: *So are they dispelled, not by the will of another, but by the union of the one Will with itself. And this is the function of God's teachers; to see no will as separate from their own, nor theirs as separate from God's.* It is the union of One Will that dispels illusions. To see no will as separate is to end the separation, which ends sickness. The function of God's teacher is to realize this non-duality of Will. In the next chapter, we will return to the issue of the oneness of Will. Many wills mean conflict. One Will is how we are one.

> **Healing is the change of mind that the Holy Spirit in the patient's mind is seeking for him. And it is the Holy Spirit in the mind of the giver Who gives the gift to him. (M-6.4:3-4)**

Who heals whom? The answer is in the above quote. True healing is of the mind; it is a change of mind that the Holy Spirit, already present in the patient's mind, is seeking. The Holy Spirit in the healer's mind joins the Holy Spirit in the patient's mind. Healing is a gift from the Holy Spirit to the Holy Spirit. Or, as Jesus puts it, from *God to God.*

> **Given by God to God, who in this holy exchange can receive less than everything? (M-6.4:12)**

Share in Healing or Share in Sickness

There is another important teaching about the cause of sickness and how healing happens in Chapter 28 of the *Text*:

> **No mind is sick until another mind agrees that they are separate. And thus it is their joint decision to be sick. (T-28.III.2:1-2)**

We can join in healing or join in sickness. Jesus already established sickness as a decision. Here He teaches that sickness is a *joint* decision. It may seem rather complicated how this works. In order for a mind to project its guilt, or be sick, it needs agreement from another mind:

> **If you withhold agreement and accept the part you play in making sickness real, the other mind cannot project its guilt without your aid in letting it perceive itself as separate and apart from you. Thus is the body not perceived as sick by both your minds from separate points of view. (T-28.III.2:3-4)**

What role do I play in making sickness real? If I agree with anyone that she is sick, I help make sickness real. We need to be in agreement that someone is sick, in order for her to be sick. If the body is perceived as sick from two different points of view, then it is sick. Healers know not to join in agreeing that sickness is real.

> **Uniting with a brother's mind prevents the cause of sickness and perceived effects. Healing is the effect of minds that join, as sickness comes from minds that separate. (T-28.III.2:5-6)**

Joining minds or separating minds are both joint decisions. This is the consensus reality.

> **Do not allow your brother to be sick, for if he is, have you abandoned him to his own dream by sharing it with him... Thus are you joined in sickness... (T-28.III.3:3;5)**

We go to Heaven together or we go to hell together.

> **Brother, you need forgiveness of your brother, for you will**
> **share in madness or in Heaven together. And you and he will**
> **raise your eyes in faith together, or not at all.**
> **(T-19.IV.D.12:7-8)**

I can choose to share in madness or share in Heaven, share in separation or share in Union. In the Kingdom everything is shared because sharing is how all graces increase. Love grows by sharing it. Peace grows by sharing it. Joy grows by sharing it. When I share these blessings I do not lose them; I increase them. How do I get more? By giving it away. This is not the world's economy where one gains by taking from another. The reverse is true as well. Sharing sickness, guilt, and death increases illusions.

When I join with a sister, I do not join with her dreams, including her dream of sickness. I will to join minds with her, as she is, still as God created Her: holy, loving, perfectly Whole, no different than me, and sharing the same, single need. What need do we share? The one need is described in various ways. It is the need to awaken from the dream, the need to return to the Kingdom of Heaven and join in the song of prayer, the need to realize that we are one because we share One Will, the need to understand that we are still as God created us, the need to accept the Atonement, the need for forgiveness and healing, the need to choose again, this time for the Holy Spirit, the need to remember the wholeness of holiness and healing.

Before the wedding is the divorce. Really? I thought the wedding was before the divorce. Before the spiritual wedding joining the mind into Christ I divorce the ego. Because the ego is not real, it is more of an annulment than a divorce. How could anti-Christ and Christ coexist? Only in a schizophrenic (split mind) dream.

> **It is the sharing of the evil dreams of hate and malice,**
> **bitterness and death, of sin and suffering and pain and**

loss, that makes them real. Unshared, they are perceived as meaningless. (T-28.V.2:1-2)

If a sister dreams she is sick, I do not share her dreams, but I join with her mind, the truth of her Identity, that I share with her.

> Thus you separate the dreamer from the dream, and join in one, but let the other go. The dream is but illusion in the mind. And with the mind you would unite, but never with the dream. (T-28.IV.2:5-7)

Egos are not joined because ego is the opposite of joining by definition. Ego is separation. I suppose egos join to kill and this egoic marriage is called the military industrial complex. Its motto is conquer, divide, and destroy. The ego is recruiting for it's army. Do not join it.

> Who shares a dream must be the dream he shares, because by sharing is a cause produced. (T-28.IV.5:5)

When I join in sharing a sister's dream of sickness I am sick as well *because by sharing is a cause produced.* In the Gospel it is stated as *When two or more are gathered together in one purpose.*

In truth, all is shared including Heaven or hell, sickness or wellness, truth or illusion, being and identity. The teaching about sharing is repeated many times in the course:

> But it is given you to know that God's function is yours, and happiness cannot be found apart from Your joint Will. (T-11.V.12:4)

> *When I am healed I am not healed alone. And I would share my healing with the world, that sickness may be banished from the mind of God's one Son, Who is my only Self.* (W-pI.137.14:3-4)

*When I am healed I am not healed alone. And I would bless
my brothers, for I would be healed with them, as they are
healed with me.* (W-pI.137.15:5-6)

Healing reflects our joint will. This is obvious when you
consider what healing is for. Healing is the way in which the
separation is overcome. Separation is overcome by union.
It cannot be overcome by separating. The decision to unite
must be unequivocal, or the mind itself is divided and not
whole. Your mind is the means by which you determine your
own condition, because mind is the mechanism of decision.
It is the power by which you separate or join, and experience
pain or joy accordingly. (T-8.IV.5:1-8)

The decision to unite must be unequivocal. That means this decision
to unite is clear, explicit, unambiguous, unmistakable, indisputable,
definite, obvious, and undeniable.

Remember always that your Identity is shared, and that Its
sharing is Its reality. (T-9.IV.1:6)

Being is known by sharing. Because God shared His Being
with you, you can know Him. (T-7.XI.7:6-7)

This is why God created us. *Divine Abstraction takes joy in sharing.*
    What about when it seems like a healing does not happen? Jesus
gives the same answer as He did to the question about when prayer
seems to fail. Healing cannot be accepted if it results in fear, and it
might do that, depending on the patient.

Yet what if the patient uses sickness as a way of life, believing
healing is the way to death? When this is so, a sudden healing
might precipitate intense depression, and a sense of loss
so deep that the patient might even try to destroy himself.

Having nothing to live for, he may ask for death. Healing must wait, for his protection. (M-6.1:6-9)

Jesus also reminds healers about the time factor.

Healing will always stand aside when it would be seen as threat. The instant it is welcome it is there. Where healing has been given it will be received. And what is time before the gifts of God? (M-6.2:1-4)

When a patient can welcome a healing without fear is not up to healers.

No teacher of God should feel disappointed if he has offered healing and it does not appear to have been received. It is not up to him to judge when his gift should be accepted. Let him be certain it has been received, and trust that it will be accepted when it is recognized as a blessing and not a curse. (M-6.2:7-9)

If a healing is given, the healer should be certain that the patient received the healing. There is no need to repeat healing if the healing seems to fail because each gift of healing is a miraculous and maximal extension of Love. There may be a delay before the patient can accept the healing, already received, without fear. The healer does not evaluate the outcome of healing and is not concerned with the time factor.

No one can give if he is concerned with the result of giving. (M-6.3:4)

One of the most difficult temptations to recognize is that to doubt a healing because of the appearance of continuing symptoms is a mistake in the form of lack of trust. (M-7.4:1)

In time there can be a great lag between the offering and the acceptance of healing. (P-3.II.10:9)

Next in *The Song Of Prayer* Jesus repeats a major teaching of the course about ceasing judgment, and the consequences if I don't stop this hateful attack on others:

> Never forget this; it is you who are God's Son, and as you choose to be to him so are you to yourself, and God to you. Nor will your judgment fail to reach to God, for you will give the role to Him you see in His creation. Do not choose amiss, or you will think that it is you who are creator in His place, and He is then no longer Cause but only an effect. Now healing is impossible, for He is blamed for your deception and your guilt. He Who is Love becomes the source of fear, for only fear can now be justified. Vengeance is His. His great destroyer, death. And sickness, suffering and grievous loss become the lot of everyone on earth, which He abandoned to the devil's care, swearing He will deliver it no more. (S-3.IV.5:1-8)

Judgment is a decision of the mind for sickness. Jesus starts off cautioning us not to forget our true, shared Identity and repeats the teaching that giving and receiving are the same. Whatever I give to a sister is what I receive. If I give forgiveness, I receive forgiveness. If I give healing, I receive healing. If I attack a sister with judgment, so am I judged. The same teaching is in the Gospels: judge not, lest ye be judged, and forgive me my lack of love as I forgive those looking for love. This is also the teaching that I pray only for myself, I forgive only myself, and I heal only myself, because, Sisters-Я-Us; we are one.

Jesus asks us to never forget this: *it is you who are God's Son, and as you choose to be to him so are you to yourself, and God to you.* If I choose to judge a sister a sinner, then I will see God as the just judge handing out punishment. Then I fall into fear instead of Love, and the three graces that are the subject of *The Song Of Prayer*, prayer, forgiveness, and healing, will elude me and I end up with ego prayers, forgiveness-to-destroy, and healing-for-separation. This is also expressed in the New Testament: whatever I do to anyone, I do to Christ, and thus I do to myself. When I realize this, judgment is easier to give up.

When I see anyone as less than innocent, I will see God as the punisher of sins. If I make sin real, I must fear God, and become lost in the dream: *Nor will your judgment fail to reach to God, for you will give the role to Him you see in His creation.* If I make this mistake, it means I joined with the ego, and follow the ego's plan to usurp the power of God by flipping truth upside down. I become maker of an anthropomorphic and vengeful god that I must fear indeed. In this case, I make myself cause, and God an effect. I go back to making God in my own image, instead of the other way around: *Do not choose amiss, or you will think that it is you who are creator in His place, and He is then no longer Cause but only an effect.*

If I make this mistake of judging, true healing cannot happen because I lost sight of the cause of sickness, which is actually separation from God, and forgot the consequences of desiring separation, including wanting to replace God and take Its throne. Instead of recognizing the true cause of illness, I place blame on God as the cause of sickness. I confuse ego and God, making God out to be the accuser and punisher of sin. Yet as Jesus teaches, healing cannot happen unless the true cause is understood and healed. *Now healing is impossible, for He is blamed for your deception and your guilt.* And then the tragic consequences of this mistake pile up. The Source of Love is twisted into the source of fear. God wants revenge and He will get it: I will die, and then, hell. *He Who is Love becomes the source of fear, for only fear can now be justified. Vengeance is His. His great destroyer, death.*

And so the ego rubs her bloody hands together with a sick smile and smacks her burnt and cracked lips as her fiction is proved fact, and death is the evidence: because of sin, God abandoned us forever to the ego's kingdom of fear and suffering: *And sickness, suffering and grievous loss become the lot of everyone on earth, which He abandoned to the devil's care, swearing He will deliver it no more.* If I join with the ego, I join with hell, with no exit, until I divorce the ego and join Jesus.

After presenting *such twisted thoughts* of the ego, our Father speaks gentle and loving thoughts:

> Come unto Me, My children, once again, without such twisted thoughts upon your hearts. You still are holy with the Holiness which fathered you in perfect sinlessness, and still surrounds you with the Arms of peace. Dream now of healing. Then arise and lay all dreaming down forever. You are he your Father loves, who never left his home, nor wandered in a savage world with feet that bleed, and with a heavy heart made hard against the love that is the truth in you. Give all your dreams to Christ and let Him be your Guide to healing, leading you in prayer beyond the sorry reaches of the world. (S-3.IV.6:1-6)

Because of the term *My children* this is the Father speaking now. He calls the ego's logic of the previous paragraph twisted and false: *Come unto Me, My children, once again, without such twisted thoughts upon your hearts.* He reminds us of the Truth: we are still as sinless and as perfect as He created us: *You still are holy with the Holiness which fathered you in perfect sinlessness, and still surrounds you with the Arms of peace.* Do we want Arms of peace or arms of war? Without conflict, the ego gets bored pretty quick. We choose what we want. Desire is prayer of the heart, 24/7.

Another major teaching of the course is summarized. This world is not real; it is like a dream. The slaughter house world is a nasty dream of death, a grim fairy tale. Before we return to Heaven we shift from the sad dream to the happy dream. The happy dream is still an illusion and involves perception, but it provides a gentler transition to Heaven, where all dreaming is shined away: *Dream now of healing* (duality). *Then arise and lay all dreaming down forever* (non-duality). Healing and forgiveness are dream events, but important dream events that permit us to shine away all dreaming *forever*. Dream events are used by the Holy Spirit as our classroom until we graduate. This is why a human birth is precious. I can only escape the dream while I am in the dream. There is no need for dreaming in Heaven.

The Father continues to remind us of the truth about His Love: *You are he your Father loves*, and how the detour into fear, the fall into separation, where we seem to suffer, is only a blind and ignorant dream of death because God does not know of separation. In truth, I am one *who never left his home* (reality), because ideas leave not their Source, *nor wandered in a savage world with feet that bleed* (dream). If I believe the ego's lies, I experience what appears to be real effects of that belief: I wander the earth *with a heavy heart made hard against the love that is the truth in me.*

The Father reminds us again of the solution, if we forget the Truth, as He does many times, each time using different words: *Give all your dreams to Christ and let Him be your Guide to healing.* We give all our dreams to Christ Who is our Guide in healing. In prayer, He leads us *beyond the sorry reaches of the world.*

In the next paragraph God the Father continues speaking. The first sentence explains how the Father is speaking: *He comes for Me and speaks My Word to you.* The pronoun *He* appears to be referring to the *Christ* from the previous sentence. Normally that role, speaking for God, is the Holy Spirit's. There is an important lesson here for course students. Words like Jesus, Christ, Holy Spirit, and God are symbols twice removed. The word Jesus is not *Him as He is.* Do not get hung up on words, which are form. The content is what is important. Jesus is the manifestation of the Holy Spirit, and they are one.

> **He comes for Me and speaks My Word to you. I would recall My weary Son to Me from dreams of malice to the sweet embrace of everlasting Love and perfect peace. My Arms are open to the Son I love, who does not understand that he is healed, and that his prayers have never ceased to sing his joyful thanks in unison with all creation, in the holiness of Love. Be still an instant. Underneath the sounds of harsh and bitter striving and defeat there is a Voice that speaks to you**

of Me. Hear this an instant and you will be healed. Hear this an instant and you have been saved. (S-3.IV.7:1-7)

I read the first sentence above as, Christ (or the Holy Spirit) *comes for Me* (the Father) *and speaks My Word.* The upper case *Me* and *My* is the Father because of the next sentence: *My Arms are open to the Son I love.* We are not the children of Christ. Jesus is brother and sister to everyone. Together we are the Christ. Nor are we the child of the Holy Spirit. Yet the Holy Spirit is the Communication Link between us and God. The *He* from the first sentence *speaks My Word to you.* I interpret this content as coming from the Father's intention and then translated into words I can understand, through either the Christ or the Holy Spirit. Therefore, in this case, Christ or the Holy Spirit is speaking for the Father *as if* in the first person, because we already learned that God does not understand words or symbols and the Holy Spirit is the translator.

God the Father "says" to me, through Christ or the Holy Spirit: *My Arms are open to the Son I love, who does not understand that he is healed.* From the Father's view, He speaks of one Son: *the Son I love,* not son's. In the dream, I was fooled to eat the forbidden fruit and thus *do not understand* that I am already healed and that I *never ceased to sing his joyful thanks in unison with all creation, in the holiness of Love.*

How is it that I am climbing the ladder of prayer to return to prayer as it is in Heaven and at the same time I *never ceased* this prayer? Again, beware level confusion. From the view of Heaven or non-duality, I never left Heaven (and hence it is a *journey without a distance*). From the earthly, dualistic view, I left Heaven and now I am climbing back. But this exit from Heaven did not happen because it could not happen. That is the meaning of the Atonement. I only dreamt it did. But because I believe the dream is reality, I become stuck in the mud. The more I struggle to get unstuck, the deeper I sink into the quicksand sewer. I can't get out by myself; I need help, a holy intervention, a real rescue, a holy tow truck to pull me inside out, with the license plate: H. S.

The Father continues to speak in a way that acknowledges our situation: *Underneath the sounds of harsh and bitter striving and defeat there is a Voice that speaks to you of Me.* The *sounds of harsh and bitter striving* refer to this world. The Voice that speaks to us of the Father is the Holy Spirit, as Jesus teaches many times. In order to hear this Voice, we are advised: *Be still an instant.* This is a call to the stillness and silence of receptive prayer, so that we can hear Him.

The last two lines tells us the fruit of this still, listening, receptive prayer, and I prefer to read it poetically:

Hear this an instant and you will be healed.

Hear this an instant and you have been saved.

What is the "this" I hear for an instant? The Voice for God, otherwise called, The Holy Spirit, Who speaks to us of the Father: *there is a Voice that speaks to you of Me.* The two verses above present an interesting time bender. When I listen to the Holy Spirit I *have been saved*, and yet I *will be healed*. This could mean that God has already given the gift of salvation and I have received it. Yet I will not be healed until I accept the grace given. In ACIM time is not linear.

In the next paragraph, the Father continues to speak through Christ or the Holy Spirit. Healers are holy helpers and now the Father asks us to help Him wake everyone: *Help Me to wake My children from the dream*, and He gives an apt description of the dream: the nightmare *of retribution and a little life beset with fear, that ends so soon it might as well have never been.*

Help Me to wake My children from the dream of retribution and a little life beset with fear, that ends so soon it might as well have never been. Let Me instead remind you of eternity, in which your joy grows greater as your love extends along with Mine beyond infinity, where time and distance have no meaning. While you wait in sorrow Heaven's melody is incomplete, because your song is part of the eternal harmony

of love. Without you is creation unfulfilled. Return to Me Who never left My Son. Listen, My child, your Father calls to you. Do not refuse to hear the Call for Love. Do not deny to Christ what is His Own. Heaven is here and Heaven is your home. (S-3.IV.8:1-9)

He compares this pitiful dualistic dream with a description of non-dual awakening: *Let Me instead remind you of eternity, in which your joy grows greater as your love extends along with Mine beyond infinity, where time and distance have no meaning.* Then He switches back to the unhappy dream: *While you wait in sorrow Heaven's melody is incomplete, because your song is part of the eternal harmony of love. Without you is creation unfulfilled.* Again, as a student of ACIM I learn to hold two ideas in mind that might seem contradictory. On the one hand, *Heaven's melody is incomplete*, and *Without you is creation unfulfilled.* On the other hand, *his prayers have never ceased to sing his joyful thanks in unison with all creation, in the holiness of Love.*

In fact, continuing the musical metaphor, Jesus teaches that the song of prayer did not miss a single note because of the dream detour into fear.

The tiny instant you would keep and make eternal, passed away in Heaven too soon for anything to notice it had come. What disappeared too quickly to affect the simple knowledge of the Son of God can hardly still be there, for you to choose to be your teacher. Only in the past,–an ancient past, too short to make a world in answer to creation,–did this world appear to rise. So very long ago, for such a tiny interval of time, that not one note in Heaven's song was missed. Yet in each unforgiving act or thought, in every judgment and in all belief in sin, is that one instant still called back, as if it could be made again in time. You keep an ancient memory before your eyes. And he who lives in memories alone is unaware of where he is. (T-26.V.5:1-7)

The Atonement was given at the same instant I forgot to laugh at the mad idea to leave God. God is not in time and cannot wait, or procrastinate, as I do in time. I learn that both these statements are "true": the song is incomplete and the song never ceased, depending on the viewpoint, Heaven's or this world's. Since I view it from this world, I *do not understand* that the song never ceased and that the separation never happened. And I can continue to believe in separation and act in unforgiving ways that recall the ancient memory of guilt. How do I get stuck in duality? I doom myself to duality because *in each unforgiving act or thought, in every judgment and in all belief in sin, is that one instant still called back, as if it could be made again in time.* That one instant is the instant of separation that lasted less than an instant, yet I can keep recalling it by acting and thinking like an ego.

Next is a sentence that contains both levels in a few words: *Return to Me Who never left My Son.* Return to Me (level two, dream or duality), Who never left (level one, reality, or non-duality). There is a certain genius in being able to consistently construct these teachings, over and over again, that go back and forth between the absolute and the relative. I think of it as like a Zen koan. There is not a satisfying way to understand this intellectually. Perhaps it prevents the ego's attempts to boast in arrogance "understanding" and at the same time fosters the humility of I do not know. The intellect can be frustrated into an intuitive breakthrough. For me, it means I benefit best by not simply reading the course but studying it. I go carefully and slowly over each sentence and see if it makes sense to me or not. There is no rush; this is not a race. I can be clear or confused and how long that takes is up to me. ACIM is not for speed reading. It is for Lectio Divina.

I am Christ's Own. Again, I like to read the last few lines of this paragraph poetically as sapient advice:

Do not refuse to hear the Call for Love.

Do not deny to Christ what is His Own.

Heaven is here and Heaven is your home.
(S-3.IV.8:7-9)

If I refuse to hear the *Call for Love*, then I deny Christ *what is His Own*, and I remain homeless and outside of Heaven. Heaven is where I do not refuse to hear the Call for Love and do not deny Christ His Own.

The next paragraph speaks of true release: *Creation leans across the bars of time to lift the heavy burden from the world.* This is still the Father speaking through the Holy Spirit. He asks us to lift up our hearts and greet grace. The crucifixion is over.

> Creation leans across the bars of time to lift the heavy burden from the world. Lift up your hearts to greet its advent. See the shadows fade away in gentleness; the thorns fall softly from the bleeding brow of him who is the holy Son of God. How lovely are you, child of Holiness! How like to Me! How lovingly I hold you in My Heart and in My Arms. How dear is every gift to Me that you have made, who healed My Son and took him from the cross. Arise and let My thanks be given you. And with My gratitude will come the gift first of forgiveness, then eternal peace. (S-3.IV.9:1-9)

The pain-relieving results of this release from suffering are described and include two references to the cross: *See the shadows* (sickness) *fade away in gentleness; the thorns fall softly from the bleeding brow of him who is the holy Son of God.* The second reference to the crucifixion is: *How dear is every gift to Me that you have made, who healed My Son and took him from the cross.* These references to the crucifixion apply to us all. Both refer to *him* in the lower case and *Son of God* in uppercase. One refers to duality, this world of many individuals, and one refers to the non-duality of Heaven. Together we are the Body of Christ, not bodies of Christ. This teaching tells us that we help in removing suffering from God's children, and this help is dear to the Father.

Earlier in the course, Jesus teaches that the last *"useless journey"* is already accomplished:

> **The journey to the cross should be the last "useless journey."**
> **Do not dwell upon it, but dismiss it as accomplished. If you**
> **can accept it as your own last useless journey, you are also**
> **free to join my resurrection. (T-4.in.3:1-3)**

When I accept what only seems like death, and the "death" of Jesus, as the *last useless journey*, then I am free to join His resurrection. Jesus already did this: *dismiss it as accomplished*. He proved death is illusion by His resurrection. Do I want to join the resurrection of Jesus, or continue dreaming of deadly madness? Why is this journey useless? Because it is not real; it is a dream. It is a journey without distance because we travel from the past to the present now.

Next in the above quote from *The Song Of Prayer*, the Father speaks of His Divine Love for His children in almost romantic terms: *How like to Me! How lovingly I hold you in My Heart and in My Arms. How dear is every gift to Me that you have made.* Regarding metaphors, if I think of God as holding me lovingly in Its Arms and Heart, Mother makes more sense than Father. Sure, fathers can hold babies as well as mothers, but usually it is the mother. Plus a baby can receive nourishment directly from the mother's breast whereas a father must first get the milk from the mother or a formula and give it to the baby from a bottle. Formula is twice removed from real milk. For many of us, the closest we come to experiencing selfless unconditional love happens in our relationship with our mothers. There is also the biological story that we spend nine months inside our mothers before the dream separation event called birth. Our experience with fathers is different.

Because we help liberate all from the cross through forgiveness, prayer, and healing, the Father is grateful to us: *Arise and let My thanks be given you.* The Father, our Source, tells us the effects of His thanks that He gives to everyone in two stages: *And with My gratitude will come the gift first of forgiveness, then eternal peace.* The Grace of the Father, given to all, leads to forgiveness and the fruit of forgiveness: eternal peace. Gratefulness is mutual. The Father thanks us and we thank the Father, as *The Song Of Prayer* describes from the first paragraph.

The term, *bars of time,* is significant and suggests that time is the jail. Not time itself, but our perception of time as linear, our guilty preoccupation with the past, and our fear of future penalty.

The Father concludes *The Song Of Prayer* asking us to return our *holy voice* to Him, so that the song of prayer is not silent. The Father is saying that He needs each and every one of us in order for Heaven to be Whole. The final paragraph of section, chapter, and *The Song Of Prayer*:

> So now return your holy voice to Me. The song of prayer
> is silent without you. The universe is waiting your release
> because it is its own. Be kind to it and to yourself, and then
> be kind to Me. I ask but this; that you be comforted and
> live no more in terror and in pain. Do not abandon Love.
> Remember this; whatever you may think about yourself,
> whatever you may think about the world, your Father needs
> you and will call to you until you come to Him in peace at
> last. (S-3.IV.10:1-7)

When the Father speaks: *So now return your holy voice to Me,* He is referring to our voice. The Father is referring to all our seemingly separate voices, that are needed to complete the song of prayer, and those voices are holy. *The song of prayer is silent without you.* Can you imagine a symphony orchestra with one musician?

The next line is the second time in this section that I hear a teaching that brings to mind Pierre Teilhard de Chardin and St. Paul: *The universe is waiting your release because it is its own.* I think Paul put it like this: *for the creation waits with eager longing for the revealing of the children of God.* Here the Father states that our own release is also the release of the universe, and that the universe is waiting for this release. Interpreting the word *universe* is a challenge, because I know from a previous teaching, late in the *Text*, that the physical universe is a temporary illusion that will pass away:

> **What seems eternal all will have an end. The stars will disappear, and night and day will be no more. All things that come and go, the tides, the seasons and the lives of men; all things that change with time and bloom and fade will not return. (T-29.VI.2:7-9)**

What universe is the Father talking about? I will take a stab at that question in the *Coda* below. From the same paragraph of the quote above: *Yet time waits upon forgiveness that the things of time may disappear because they have no use.* (T-29.VI.2:14) When forgiveness is complete, the need for time is over, and *the things of time*, being now re-cognized as unreal, disappear. When we graduate, the classroom is no longer needed.

Next the Father makes an interesting statement: *Be kind to it and to yourself, and then be kind to Me.* This sentence teaches two steps of kindness. First, I am kind to it (the universe) and myself, and then I am kind to the Father. The order is important as when Jesus teaches the formula for healing: first I forgive and then I pray. Therefore, it seems that I cannot extend kindness to the Father unless I first extend it to the universe and myself.

If I think like a true healer, I share the holy *Thought of God*. Healing and illness are effects of thought.

> **To heal is the only kind of thinking in this world that resembles the Thought of God, and because of the elements they share, can transfer easily to it. (T-7.II.1:1)**

Notice that healing is a *kind of thinking*. Healing is of the mind and for the mind.

Earlier in this chapter we looked at the radical teaching about the body's potential to be unlimited by age, weather, food and drink, etc. In the Psychotherapy pamphlet there is a related teaching about healers. In the context of the first miracle principal, that there is no order of difficulty in miracles or healing, Jesus teaches that few healers understand this truth and practice it: *There are some in this world who have come very close, but they have not accepted the gift entirely in order to stay and let their understanding remain on earth until the closing of time.* (P-3.II.7:5) A few more details are given. They are not professional therapists. Jesus calls them *the Saints of God* and *the Saviors of the World.* He says that *Their image remains, because they have chosen that it be so. They take the place of other images, and help with kindly dreams.* (P-3.II.7:7-10) I do not pretend to understand what that means, but I find it interesting, and I wanted to share it.

The last few lines of *The Song Of Prayer* are precious and loving. I don't think they need any commentary. Once again, I present them as poetry, iambic pentameter, ten syllables per line:

> I ask but this; that you be comforted
>
> And live no more in terror and in pain.
>
> Do not abandon Love. Remember this;
>
> Whatever you may think about yourself,
>
> Whatever you may think about the world,
>
> Your Father needs you and will call to you
>
> Until you come to Him in peace at last. (S-3.IV.10:5-7)

In summary, *The Song Of Prayer* is sharing with us an advanced lesson that was perhaps not fully covered in the previous 1250 pages of the course, and that teaching is about the relationship between prayer, forgiveness, and healing, and how to discern the difference between the false and the true versions of each. Jesus *made a clear distinction, still obscure to you, between the false and true. He offered you a final demonstration that it is impossible to kill God's Son; nor can his life in any way be changed by sin and evil, malice, fear or death.* (C-5.3:4-5)

Chapter Five

THE PRAYERS TO THE FATHER

*W*ithin ACIM Jesus teaches many prayers to the Father. The main focus in this chapter will be the prayers presented in Part II of the *Workbook*. Part II of the *Workbook* contains Lessons 221 to 365. The first 130 Lessons in Part II each contain a short prayer to the Father, and a short comment, two lessons per page. The comments stop from Lessons 351-360, and only a prayer is given. The five final Lessons, 361-365, are a little different and have their own *Introduction*. The prayers in Part II represent the true contemplative prayer that Jesus is preparing us for. The first 220 Lessons from Part I, are preparation for this Part II, that focuses on prayer to the Father. Jesus lays out His plan for His course in the first chapter of ACIM:

> A solid foundation is necessary...Some of the later steps in this course, however, involve a more direct approach to God Himself. It would be unwise to start on these steps without careful preparation, or awe will be confused with fear, and the experience will be more traumatic than beatific. Healing is of God in the end. The means are being carefully explained to you. Revelation may occasionally reveal the end to you, but to reach it the means are needed. (T-1.VII.5:1;7-11)

The *later* steps refer to Part II of the *Workbook* where we attempt a more direct approach to God.

First, students build a solid foundation of the course metaphysics. This is mind training that replaces wrong-minded thinking with right-minded thinking. This is not the goal of the course but a preparation for deeper prayer: we are being prepared for *a more direct approach to God Himself.* Jesus advises us not to attempt this more

167

direct approach without adequate preparation: It is *unwise to start on these steps without careful preparation.* The danger is confusing shock and awe.

In the *Introduction* to the *Workbook*, Jesus provides more details about how carefully ACIM is planned out:

> A theoretical foundation such as the text provides is necessary as a framework to make the exercises in this workbook meaningful. (W-in.1:1)

> The workbook is divided into two main sections, the first dealing with the undoing of the way you see now, and the second with the acquisition of true perception. (W-in.3:1)

This process of learning from Jesus is described in terms of perception. The first part is undoing false perception, *the way you see now.* My old perception sees only the past. The second part replaces false perception with true perception of the healed mind (understanding with the Mind of Christ). My new perception sees only the Now.

> The purpose of the workbook is to train your mind in a systematic way to a different perception of everyone and everything in the world. (W-in.4:1)

As students of ACIM, we are learning a different perception of everyone and everything.

One goal of ACIM is to remove the blocks to the awareness of God's Divine Love. Since fear blocks the awareness of Love, that is already and always present, Jesus designed ACIM to limit and eliminate fear, not increase it. Remember, the final obstacle to peace is the fear of God. This more direct approach to the Father will not work if we are afraid of Him, or afraid of His Will. This fear is based on the claim that we are sinful and guilty, and so we fear the just wrath of God. The means that Jesus uses to accomplish this preparation He teaches us carefully: *The means are being carefully explained to you.*

While on earth, the direct experience of God, that the course calls *revelation*, may happen, but it is not permanent. This experience gives a glimpse of the end goal; the blocks to the awareness of Divine Love are temporarily disabled and one experiences this Divine Love, that is so holy it is unspeakable. What means are being carefully explained to us? The means to reach revelation and stay there.

Aware of Jesus' plan in His course, that He *carefully* explains to us, let us look at the *Introduction* to Part II of the *Workbook*, that is *a more direct approach to God, Himself.* This *Introduction* starts with these words:

Words will mean little now. We use them but as guides on which we do not now depend. For now we seek direct experience of truth alone. (W-pII.in.1:1-3)

A major shift is taking place from prayer using words to prayer that seeks the *direct experience of truth alone.* Part I of the *Workbook* is about 400 pages long and includes 70 Lessons that are reviews of previous Lessons. That means there are 150 original Lessons and 70 reviews in 400 pages in Part I. In Part II there are 140 Lessons in 82 pages (no reviews) and the final five lessons, which are the same, take less than a half page, demonstrating an increasing reduction of the number of words used in the form of the *Workbook.* The short prayers and comments of each lesson in Part II are designed to introduce a period of silent, wordless, and receptive prayer.

The student is also asked to read, slowly, a one-page summary of a core course teaching, *themes of special relevance*, before each lesson. As there are fourteen of these, we end up slowly reading each passage ten times (over 10 days of lessons, or more if preferred), anchoring these teachings in the mind before sitting in silence. After reading one of these one-page summaries and reading the short prayer and comment for a particular lesson, we wait in silence.

There are two or three guidelines regarding doing the *Workbook*, depending on how one looks at it. Jesus says not to do no more than one lesson per day:

> **Do not undertake to do more than one set of exercises a day. (W-in.2:6)**

Although I do not do more than one lesson per day, I can give as much time as I wish to any lesson. The next rule advises how to practice the lessons: with great specificity:

> **...the exercises be practiced with great specificity, as will be indicated. This will help you to generalize the ideas involved to every situation in which you find yourself, and to everyone and everything in it. (W-in.6:1-2)**

The third guideline follows the second naturally and is similar to the second except with a subtle distinction. In applying the exercises with great specificity, we do not exclude any person, situation, or thing.

> **...be sure that you do not decide for yourself that there are some people, situations or things to which the ideas are inapplicable. (W-in.6:3)**

These lessons are to be generalized, so that we can apply them to anyone, anything, anytime, and anywhere. If we place any limits or exclusions to the lessons, full transfer of the lesson is denied. What is the purpose of these lessons? The purpose of these lessons is *the acquisition of true perception* by training our minds in a *systematic way to a different perception of everyone and everything in the world.* This shift in perception is the switch from seeing only the past to seeing only the present, where the holy instant lives.

In the *Introduction* to Part II of the *Workbook*, Jesus describes this numinous prayer in several ways, but most often as waiting for the Father, after welcoming the Father to come:

...we leave the world of pain, and go to enter peace. (W-pII.in.1:4)

...we wait in quiet expectation for our God and Father. (W-pII.in.2:2)

...now we wait for Him. We will continue spending time with Him each morning and at night, as long as makes us happy. (W-pII.in.2:5-6)

We say some simple words of welcome, and expect our Father to reveal Himself, as He has promised. (W-pII.in.3:3)

Now do we come to Him with but His Word upon our minds and hearts, and wait for Him to take the step to us that He has told us, through His Voice, He would not fail to take when we invited Him. (W-pII.in.4:1)

We say the words of invitation that His Voice suggests, and then we wait for Him to come to us. (W-pII.in.4:6)

Sit silently and wait upon your Father. (W-pII.in.5:5)

And now we wait in silence, unafraid and certain of Your coming. (W-pII.in.7:1)

The last quote above is a little different because it is expressed as a prayer to the Father. This *Introduction* is mostly instruction for how to do the final 140 Lessons of Part II, as we see above. Yet Jesus breaks into prayer in the sixth paragraph:

Father, we give these holy times to You, in gratitude to Him Who taught us how to leave the world of sorrow in exchange for its replacement, given us by You. (W-pII.in.6:2)

> **For in this final section, we need only call to God, and all temptations disappear. Instead of words, we need but feel His Love. (W-pII.in.10:2-3)**

These ideas about prayer in the *Introduction* to Part II of the *Workbook* demonstrate that this is a contemplative form of prayer, using words minimally to invite the Father, and then waiting for Him to reveal Himself as He chooses. This is not prayer in the *usual sense*.

Again, it will be difficult to approach the Father this way if we are afraid of Him. In that case, we experience fear rather than awe in His presence. Hence the importance of the *solid foundation* in preparation for this. The time one gives to God in silent prayer is *holy time*.

These prayers to the Father, given to us by Jesus, are translated by the Holy Spirit so that the Father understands our intention and invitation to Him. All the prayers in the *Workbook* Part II are italicized, but not all the prayers in the *Text*. In true prayer we seek peace in silence. Here is the first prayer from Part II:

> *Father, I come to You today to seek the peace that You alone can give. I come in silence. In the quiet of my heart, the deep recesses of my mind, I wait and listen for Your Voice. My Father, speak to me today. I come to hear Your Voice in silence and in certainty and love, sure You will hear my call and answer me. (W-pII.221.1:1-5)*

Notice the identifying features of this prayer: *I come in silence; in the quiet of my heart; the deep recesses of my mind; I wait and listen; I come to hear Your Voice in silence and in certainty and love.* What are we seeking? The peace that comes from God only. The title of Lesson 221 is *Peace to my mind. Let all my thoughts be still.* This idea suggests that peace of mind comes when I allow *all my thoughts to be still.* In the short commentary after this prayer, contemplative ideas are repeated:

> **Now do we wait in quiet. God is here, because we wait together. (W-pII.221.2:1-2)**

Who do we wait with in silence and stillness? We wait with Jesus or the Holy Spirit. We pray with Jesus and He speaks: *Our minds are joined.* (W-pII.221.2:5) Jesus asks us to accept *His confidence* in His Father's faithfulness. Why is God here? Because I wait with the Holy Spirit. Because we wait *together.*

In this world of duality, there appear to be billions of separate individuals, not to mention *every living thing.* But in non-dual Heaven, the Father has one Child, one Creation. This truth of both levels (though one is temporary) is expressed again in one short sentence in the prayer from Lesson 223:

For we who are Your holy Son are sinless. (W-pII.223.2:2)

It starts out with the many (duality) using the word *we* and then the prayer states that we are God's holy Son. It ends with the singular (non-duality) but started with the plural. Jesus does not say that we are God's sons, but Son. This is the truth of Heaven, but seemingly not true in this world. Together in unity we are the Father's one Child Who is sinless.

Lesson 224 offers a beautiful prayer that seems familiar to me because it is similar to a prayer by the contemplative hermit, Thomas Merton (1915-1968). Here is the prayer in Lesson 224:

My Name, O Father, still is known to You. I have forgotten It, and do not know where I am going, who I am, or what it is I do. Remind me, Father, now, for I am weary of the world I see. Reveal what You would have me see instead. (W-pII.224.2:1-4)

Are you weary of the world you see? I am. And here is Merton's prayer from his book, *Thoughts In Solitude* (1956):

My Lord God, I have no idea where I am going. I do not see the road ahead of me. I cannot know for certain where it will end. Nor do I really know myself, and the fact that I think I am

following your will does not mean that I am actually doing so.
But I believe that the desire to please you does in fact please
you. And I hope I have that desire in all that I am doing. I
hope that I will never do anything apart from that desire.
And I know that if I do this you will lead me by the right road,
though I may know nothing about it. Therefore will I trust
you always though I may seem to be lost and in the shadow of
death. I will not fear, for you are ever with me, and you will
never leave me to face my perils alone.

Jesus teaches the same ideas earlier in ACIM, though more as a statement of our identity-confused condition than as a prayer:

I do not know the thing I am, and therefore do not know
what I am doing, where I am, or how to look upon the world
or on myself. (T-31.V.17:7)

Although the quote above is true, it can also be frightening for us because it threatens the self-made self-concept that we identify with, even though this self-concept is not our true Identity.

The major themes of these 145 prayers from Part II of the *Workbook* include present perception, peace, forgiveness, hearing God's Voice (the Holy Spirit), Identity as Christ, unity and/or union, Love, sinlessness, holiness, thanksgiving, remembering God, Heaven, responsibility, the foolishness of fear, joy, salvation, humility, open-mindedness, releasing judgment, non-interference, sharing, trust, equality, truth, only God, Source or Cause, purity, Christ's vision, and Will (especially the unity of the Father's Will with His Child's will). Usually more than one of these themes is presented in each prayer. For this final chapter the focus is on the theme of Will and below I present several prayers that include the theme of Will. If you want to find the prayers with a different theme, like peace, or identity, you can do this yourself. You simply pick a theme and then identify and collect the prayers that apply to that theme.

The idea that Reality is non-dual is hard to understand in this world. It is simply beyond the current limits of understanding. It is a different dimension called Heaven. Intellectual or verbal attempts to understand non-duality fail; they are *raids on the unspeakable.* Nor do we need to understand it now. We will experience it when we are ready. That said, I prefer to consider non-duality in terms of Will. Non-duality is where the Daughter's will is *one* with the Father's Will, ending the suffering of conflict caused by opposing wills. The Father and Child share one Will, just as we share one Voice in the song of prayer. If someone thinks that they have a separate will that is different from God's Will, they will experience guilt and fear as a consequence of this conflict.

Early in the *Text* Jesus urges us to be free of this conflict, and this gets to the heart of what delays our return to Heaven: the resistance to giving up a seemingly separate and independent will, because we view this surrender of self as a serious sacrifice of unique individuality. I want to be my own boss even though so far this stubborn bossiness has not led to peace or union or Love. This conflict is an inner conflict within the mind. I wrote about this already in *God Is* and I am repeating a relevant quote from the sixth section of Chapter Two in the *Text* called *Fear and Conflict* because it relates to God's Will and our willingness. I am also repeating it because Jesus says this lesson is *particularly apt to be overlooked. I will therefore repeat it, urging you to listen:*

> The Holy Spirit cannot ask more than you are willing to do. The strength to do comes from your undivided decision. There is no strain in doing God's Will as soon as you recognize that it is also your own. The lesson here is quite simple, but particularly apt to be overlooked. I will therefore repeat it, urging you to listen. Only your mind can produce fear. It does so whenever it is conflicted in what it wants, producing inevitable strain because wanting and doing are

discordant. This can be corrected only by accepting a unified goal. (T-2.VI.6:2-9)

The Holy Spirit works with us according to our willingness. She never forces anything but waits on us to be willing and defenseless. A little willingness is all Jesus asks us for. Yet without that willingness we limit what the Holy Spirit can do with us. The Holy Spirit respects human will. She *cannot ask more than you are willing to do.* The non-duality of One Will is described above in two phrases: *undivided decision* and *unified goal.* If the Holy Spirit asked me to do something that I am unwilling to do, more guilt and fear would result and that is the last thing the Holy Spirit intends.

When someone believes that her own will is in conflict with God's Will, the result is fear because this conflict is seen as sin, that causes guilt, that causes fear. Later in the same chapter Jesus explains the importance of freeing ourselves from this fear and conflict *quickly* if we are to become miracle-minded:

If a sufficient number become truly miracle-minded, this shortening process can be virtually immeasurable. It is essential, however, that you free yourself from fear quickly, because you must emerge from the conflict if you are to bring peace to other minds. (T-2.VIII.2:7-8)

If one wills to be a teacher or healer of God, and shorten the time of suffering, one must *emerge from the conflict.* We are free of the conflict when the seemingly separated will is *undivided* from God's Will and *unified* with God's Will. With both the ego and the Holy Spirit in the split mind, conflict happens.

In ACIM, Jesus teaches that the idea or perception that our will is in conflict with God's Will is an illusion, and many of the prayers in Part II reflect this. Even though the separate and individual will is an illusion, we can still believe, and even insist, that the so-called autonomous will is real. Our real will is only sleeping:

The Holy Spirit is the motivation for miracle-mindedness; the decision to heal the separation by letting it go. Your will is still in you because God placed it in your mind, and although you can keep it asleep you cannot obliterate it. God Himself keeps your will alive by transmitting it from His Mind to yours as long as there is time. The miracle itself is a reflection of this union of Will between Father and Son. (T-5.II.1:4-7)

Although we can keep our will asleep, we cannot lose it or destroy it. God placed this will in our mind and He keeps it alive. How does the Father keep our sleeping will alive? *By transmitting it from His Mind to* ours, as long as our exile in the hot and dry desert of time continues. The prayers collected below sometimes acknowledge our confused thinking about will and Will. What mirrors the miracle itself? The *union of Will between Father and Son.*

I think it is perfectly okay to substitute the word *Mother* for the word, *Father,* and ex-change masculine pronouns for feminine ones, and substitute *sister* for *brother* and *Daughter* for *Son.* In fact, if your own human father was abusive, neglectful, or absent, I recommend that you do just that. If both your parents were unable to be good parents, you can try any word or symbol that works for you. Instead of Father or Mother you could use Friend, Source, Lord, God, or Spirit. Do not confuse form with content. The words, Mother or Father are form, not content. Choose any word or symbol that represents unconditional love or truth or holiness to you. If the quote is italicized, it is a prayer. If the quote is not italicized, it is a comment on a prayer, usually from the same lesson. For this first prayer related to Will both gender versions of Lesson 227 are presented:

Mother, it is today that I am free, because my will is Yours.
I thought to make another will. Yet nothing that I thought
apart from You exists. And I am free because I was mistaken,

and did not affect my own reality at all by my illusions. Now I give them up, and lay them down before the feet of truth, to be removed forever from my mind. This is my holy instant of release. Mother, I know my will is one with Yours.

Father, it is today that I am free, because my will is Yours. I thought to make another will. Yet nothing that I thought apart from You exists. And I am free because I was mistaken, and did not affect my own reality at all by my illusions. Now I give them up, and lay them down before the feet of truth, to be removed forever from my mind. This is my holy instant of release. Father, I know my will is one with Yours. (W-pII.227.1:1-7)

Father, I give You all my thoughts today. I would have none of mine. In place of them, give me Your Own. I give You all my acts as well, that I may do Your Will instead of seeking goals which cannot be obtained, and wasting time in vain imaginings. Today I come to You. I will step back and merely follow You. (W-pII.233.1:1-6)

I will accept the way You choose for me to come to You, my Father. For in that will I succeed, because it is Your Will. And I would recognize that what You will is what I will as well, and only that. And so I choose to love Your Son. Amen. (W-pII.246.2:1-5)

You are the Self Whom You created Son, creating like Yourself and One with You. My Self, which rules the universe, is but Your Will in perfect union with my own, which can but offer glad assent to Yours, that it may be extended to Itself. (W-pII.253.2:1-2)

Father, today I would but hear Your Voice. In deepest silence I would come to You, to hear Your Voice and to receive Your Word. I have no prayer but this: I come to You to ask You for the truth. And truth is but Your Will, which I would share with You today. (W-pII.254.1:1-4)

Father, forgiveness is Your chosen means for our salvation. Let us not forget today that we can have no will but Yours. And thus our purpose must be Yours as well, if we would reach the peace You will for us. (W-pII.257.2:1-3)

Father, Your Will is mine, and only that. There is no other will for me to have. Let me not try to make another will, for it is senseless and will cause me pain. Your Will alone can bring me happiness, and only Yours exists. If I would have what only You can give, I must accept Your Will for me, and enter into peace where conflict is impossible, Your Son is one with You in being and in will, and nothing contradicts the holy truth that I remain as You created me. (W-pII.307.1:1-5)

And with this prayer we enter silently into a state where conflict cannot come, because we join our holy will with God's, in recognition that they are the same. (W-pII.307.2:1)

Within me is eternal innocence, because it is God's Will that it be there forever and forever. I, His Son, whose will is limitless as is His Own, can will no change in this. For to deny my Father's Will is to deny my own. To look within is but to find my will as God created it, and as it is. I fear to look within because I think I made another will that is not true, and made it real. Yet it has no effects. Within me is the Holiness of God. Within me is the memory of Him. (W-pII.309.1:1-8)

*Father, Your Will is total. And the goal which stems from it
shares its totality. What aim but the salvation of the world
could You have given me? And what but this could be the Will
my Self has shared with You?* (W-pII.319.2:1-4)

*Your Will can do all things in me, and then extend to all the
world as well through me. There is no limit on Your Will. And
so all power has been given to Your Son.* (W-pII.320.2:1-3)

I am he in whom the power of my Father's Will abides.
(W-pII.320.1:6)

As demonstrated by these quotes, the issue of will and the union of
God's Will and His Child's will is a major theme of the prayers in Part
II of the *Workbook*. I appreciate how consistent Jesus is over several
different lessons.

Here are two sentences from the prayer in Lesson 326 that make
a powerful statement of non-duality.

*Where You established me I still abide. And all Your
attributes abide in me, because it is Your Will to have a Son so
like his Cause that Cause and Its Effect are indistinguishable.*
(W-pII.326.1:4-5)

God is Cause and we are Effect. Yet it is God's will that we be so much
like Him that the difference between us is *indistinguishable! All* of the
Father's attributes abide in us although some of these may be sleeping.

*There is no will but Yours. And I am glad that nothing I
imagine contradicts what You would have me be. It is Your
Will that I be wholly safe, eternally at peace. And happily
I share that Will which You, my Father, gave as part of me.*
(W-pII.328.2:1-4)

God's Will is the only Will there is: non-duality. Non-dual-will.

Here is the full Lesson 329, *I have already chosen what You will*, with the prayer followed by the comment. In this prayer Jesus says that our Identity is God's Will.

> *Father, I thought I wandered from Your Will, defied it, broke its laws, and interposed a second will more powerful than Yours. Yet what I am in truth is but Your Will, extended and extending. This am I, and this will never change. As You are One, so am I one with You. And this I chose in my creation, where my will became forever one with Yours. That choice was made for all eternity. It cannot change, and be in opposition to itself. Father, my will is Yours. And I am safe, untroubled and serene, in endless joy, because it is Your Will that it be so.* (W-pII.329.1:1-9)

> Today we will accept our union with each other and our Source. We have no will apart from His, and all of us are one because His Will is shared by all of us. Through it we recognize that we are one. Through it we find our way at last to God. (W-pII.329.2:1-4)

In Lesson 329 above, *how* we are one is described in terms of shared Will: *all of us are one because His Will is shared by all of us.*

> *There is no will except the Will of Love. Fear is a dream, and has no will that can conflict with Yours. Conflict is sleep, and peace awakening. Death is illusion; life, eternal truth. There is no opposition to Your Will. There is no conflict, for my will is Yours.* (W-pII.331.1:6-11)

> *Father, I want what goes against my will, and do not want what is my will to have. Straighten my mind, my Father. It is sick...I do not know my will, but He is sure it is Your Own.*

*And He will speak for me, and call Your miracles to come to
me.* (W-pII.347.1:1-3;10-11)

Who is the He mentioned twice in the prayer above? He is the Holy
Spirit. We resist giving up the illusion of freedom that a private and
independent will seems to provide. We only need willingness to surrender the illusionary little will. How it happens is up to God. There
is no sacrifice because we only surrender illusions of independence,
self-will, uniqueness, and freedom. Although how this happens is not
up to us, when it happens might be. One Will happens when we are
willing and defenseless. The heartfelt desire for this reunion is the
willingness and prayer for this union.

The last five lessons have their own *Introduction* which starts in
a similar way as the *Introduction* to Part II:

**Our final lessons will be left as free of words as possible.
(W-fl.in.1:1)**

**To Him we leave these lessons, as to Him we give our lives
henceforth. (W-fl.in.1:4)**

The *Him* two times above is the Holy Spirit. To Her we give our lives
and to Her we leave these final five lessons. The final lines of this
Introduction are precious and loving:

**Would He hurt His Son? Or would He rush to answer him,
and say, "This is My Son, and all I have is his"? Be certain He
will answer thus, for these are His Own words to you. And
more than that can no one ever have, for in these words is all
there is, and all that there will be throughout all time and in
eternity. (W-fl.in.6:2-5)**

Jesus promises that the Father's Own message to us, every one of us,
is: "*This is My Son, and all I have is his.*" We are asked to be certain
of this, the Father's Infinite Love. He gives us *everything*-all that He

has, and all that She is, and *all that there will be*... This is what the father told his older son in the parable about the prodigal son. Since the Father shares all that He has with us, why ask for more? We only need to accept what He is always giving to us. All He has is all He is, because being is having:

> If sickness is separation, the decision to heal and to be healed is the first step toward recognizing what you truly want...To unite having and being is to unite your will with His, for He wills you Himself. And you will yourself to Him because, in your perfect understanding of Him, you know there is but one Will. (T-11.II.1:1;4-5)

Our Father wills Himself to us and we will ourselves to Him because being and will are shared. When our understanding of the Father is *perfect* we *know there is but one Will.*

> Being is known by sharing. Because God shared His Being with you, you can know Him. (T-7.XI.7:6-7)

Because God shares His Being with us, we have everything: *Remember that in the Kingdom there is no difference between having and being, as there is in existence. In the state of being the mind gives everything always.* (T-4.VII.5:7-8)

The last five Lessons are the same and repeated for five days, or longer if preferred, and this prayer is also related to Will. It is a little different because this prayer is addressed to the Holy Spirit instead of the Father. The comment after the prayer is included:

> *This holy instant would I give to You.*
>
> *Be You in charge. For I would follow You,*
>
> *Certain that Your direction gives me peace.*
> (W-fl.361-365:1-3)

> And if I need a word to help me, He will give it to me. If
> I need a thought, that will He also give. And if I need but
> stillness and a tranquil, open mind, these are the gifts I will
> receive of Him. He is in charge by my request. And He will
> hear and answer me, because He speaks for God my Father
> and His holy Son. (W-fl.361-365.1:1-5)

When someone is *certain* that the Holy Spirit's direction gives her peace, she has developed the trust in God that permits surrender to the Father's Will, that she shares with Him.

That these final five lessons are addressed to the Holy Spirit, instead of the Father, like the previous 140 lessons of Part II, is significant. This emphasis on the Holy Spirit continues in the *Epilogue*, that ends the *Workbook*. This teaching about the Holy Spirit reveals how important the Holy Spirit is to everyone. In the *Epilogue*, the Holy Spirit is called, *Your Friend*, and She goes with us, because She is in us, as God's gift, our connection to the Father while we dream of duality.

Who do we give our lives henceforth to? The Holy Spirit and She *is in charge by my request.*

> All real pleasure comes from doing God's Will. This is
> because *not* doing it is a denial of Self. Denial of Self results
> in illusions, while correction of the error brings release from
> it. Do not deceive yourself into believing that you can relate
> in peace to God or to your brothers with anything external.

> Child of God, you were created to create the good, the
> beautiful and the holy. Do not forget this. The Love of God,
> for a little while, must still be expressed through one body to
> another, because vision is still so dim. You can use your body
> best to help you enlarge your perception so you can achieve
> real vision, of which the physical eye is incapable. Learning
> to do this is the body's only true usefulness.
> (T-1.VII.1:4-7;2:1-5)

CODA

J wrote this book because *The Song Of Prayer* inspired me deeply. I remain impressed and amazed by this 22-page extension of the principals of *A Course In Miracles*. This spiritual teaching is so filled with holy wisdom that I decided to share it because *Nothing real can be increased except by sharing.* (T-4.VII.5:2) And because sharing is God's Will: *Divine Abstraction takes joy in sharing.* (T-4.VII.5:4)

Except for Part II of the *Workbook*, prayer might not seem to be a major theme of ACIM. It is interesting that Jesus gave *The Song Of Prayer* and the pamphlet *Psychotherapy*, after the apparent completion of ACIM. *Psychotherapy* (25 pages) came first; *The Song Of Prayer* (22 pages) came second and is the final scribing of ACIM. It is almost, as if in hindsight, that Jesus wanted to teach something important, something that was not already covered in the course. Because of a background in monastic life, Centering Prayer, and contemplative prayer, I value this teaching dearly.

This teaching on prayer that uses the metaphor, the ladder of prayer, describes levels of prayer as the rungs on a ladder from earth to Heaven. The development of prayer can be seen as an example of the spiritual journey, just as the development of trust in God is another formula for the spiritual life found in ACIM. Jesus teaches us not only how to pray, but also how not to pray. True prayer is contingent on true forgiveness. No doubt Christians are familiar with the similar teaching of Jesus in the Gospels where He teaches that before I make a prayer-offering to God, I first go and make peace with whomever holds a grudge or grievance against me, and then make the offering to God. True forgiveness lifts its sister, prayer, up the ladder to the Father, with wings. We fertilize our growth in prayer with forgiveness, and our quality of prayer is determined according to how we are in relationship. Are you and I friends or foes?

In *The Song Of Prayer* there is repetition of major course ideas, presented briefly, but there is also, in my opinion, new teachings that supplement ACIM. Otherwise, why give this addendum to the course? I do not think Jesus gave *The Song Of Prayer* simply to repeat what He already taught because there is already much repetition before He gave us *The Song Of Prayer*. Although there is frequent teaching in ACIM about forgiveness and healing, there is little instruction in prayer. In particular, the relationship between prayer and forgiveness, and the relationship between prayer, healing, and forgiveness, is new. Jesus also presents many examples of true and false healing, true and false forgiveness, and true and false prayer. Students learn how to discern the difference between true and false, just as Jesus did. That dichotomy is part of duality, where we now seem to be, and not part of Heaven.

Also, the teaching about forgiveness is expanded. Forgiveness is a major theme of the course, certainly more so than prayer or healing. In *The Song Of Prayer* Jesus teaches us to leave the form that forgiveness takes up to Him or the Holy Spirit, and not put it in an *earthly frame*. He uses the terms *forgiveness-for-salvation, forgiveness-to-destroy, forgiveness to kill* and the word *sister* only in *The Song Of Prayer*.

The third and final chapter of *The Song Of Prayer, Healing*, emphasizes that true healing is of the mind. If the mind is healed of the guilt it believes in, then the mind can experience *pure joy* and the kind of holy death that Jesus describes in this chapter. Remember how he describes a good death: *Death is reward; a quiet choice, made joyfully and with a sense of peace; it is liberty; we go in peace to freer air and gentler climate; a kind forgiveness of the ways of earth; a gentle welcome to release; this gentle passage to a higher prayer.* Clearly, Jesus does not want us to fear death. Healing, prayer, and forgiveness work together to help us return Home. All three of these graces are necessary, yet only prayer is eternal, and it is through prayer that we might experience the direct Truth of God Himself. Yet without forgiveness, prayer cannot climb the ladder to Heaven. And without healing the mind of guilt, we will not experience the gentle death, that only *seems like death*. It is all interconnected.

There are times when a student comes across a sentence or an idea from the course that is hard to understand. We can be okay with that, not knowing. If one is not clear about a word, or passage, in the course, that is normal. It is fine and perhaps wise to admit, "I don't know." If someone does not understand something from the course, perhaps she does not really need to know what it means now. Perhaps she simply cannot understand what is yet beyond a limited level of understanding. Perhaps the resistance to the truth of What-We-Are is too strong right now.

This is quoted above but it relates to this discussion about what we need to know: ...*forgiveness has an end. For it becomes unneeded when the rising up is done. Yet now it has a purpose beyond which you cannot go, nor have you need to go.* (S-2.in.1:7-9) If we can accept our temporary ignorance humbly, then there is no need to feel discouraged or confused over ideas not understood yet. Until forgiveness is complete, it has a purpose that we cannot go beyond, nor have we need to go beyond it. *Do not, then, seek to understand what is beyond you yet...* (S-2.III.2:3) Dr. Wapnick once read a passage from the course and then said something like this: "No one here can understand what that means." This quote from the *Workbook* agrees: *There is no need to further clarify what no one in the world can understand.* (W-pI.169.10:1)

Here is an example from personal study, that now I can look back on with a chuckle. *God Is* ended with two quotes from *Workbook* Lesson 169: *By grace I Live. By grace I am released.* In the paragraph following those quotes came a sentence I did not understand:

> **We do not hasten it, in that what you will offer was concealed from Him Who teaches what forgiveness means. (W-pI.169.7:3)**

I struggled a while trying to figure it out, starting with the context. I like clarity. Eventually I set it aside as a verse I did not get. I figured it had something to do with time because of the first part: *We do not hasten it.* But the rest was a blur. Then, within a day or two of trying to understand this verse, I came across a Kenneth Wapnick comment on the exact same verse in his book about time. His comment on the verse didn't really help me. Then he added the following:

> Before we go on to that [next] paragraph, however, I want to make a few more comments about these lines. First, they are a bit tricky because they are in verse, and so a couple of words have been left out which would have made the meaning clearer. It is also difficult to understand because the paragraphing was done incorrectly.
> (Wapnick, *A Vast Illusion*, 2007, p. 43-44)

Aha! No wonder that verse was hard to figure out. There is no need for anyone to be discouraged by confusion. You simply set it aside and wait for help. The form of ACIM is not important in itself. The form is simply a means to communicate the content of ACIM. The content is what is important. Yet I am grateful for the form of the course, that is so skillfully presented. There are other ways to access the same content, but Jesus teaches the course is quicker and He gave it to save time because we are moving much too slow. ACIM came about as the fruit of a holy relationship, a labor of love.

*   *   *

Earlier in this book I promised to return to a few phrases in *The Song Of Prayer* that might challenge important ideas in the metaphysics of ACIM, such as, *There is no world*. For example: *Forgiveness shines its merciful reprieve upon each blade of grass and feathered wing and all the living things upon the earth*, and the use of the word *universe*. We return to that now. The above quote, about birds, grass, and all earthly living things echoes lines from the *Text*:

> All this beauty will rise to bless your sight as you look upon the world with forgiving eyes. For forgiveness literally transforms vision, and lets you see the real world reaching

quietly and gently across chaos, removing all illusions that
had twisted your perception and fixed it on the past. The
smallest leaf becomes a thing of wonder, and a blade of grass
a sign of God's perfection. (T-17.II.6.1-3)

What is *twisted* perception? Perception that is *fixed on the past*. Here
is another prayer from the *Text* regarding the *completed picture of
God's Son:*

I thank You, Father, knowing You will come to close each
little gap that lies between the broken pieces of Your holy
Son. Your Holiness, complete and perfect, lies in every one
of them. And they are joined because what is in one is in
them all. How holy is the smallest grain of sand, when it is
recognized as being part of the completed picture of God's
Son! The forms the broken pieces seem to take mean nothing.
For the whole is in each one. And every aspect of the Son of
God is just the same as every other part. (T-28.IV.9:1-7)

Apparently, not only the living things of the earth, but even *the smallest grain of sand* is part of the completion of God's creation. I could
call it metaphor but that might be taking the easy way out.

The forgiven world is the real world; the forgiven universe is the
real universe. That a blade of grass or the smallest grain of sand could
demonstrate God's perfection indicates a transformation of perception, as the *Workbook* intends. The blade of grass or grain of sand did
not change but one's perception sure did. In the *Text*, Jesus does give
a hint about a universe *beyond the stars:*

The power set in you in whom the Holy Spirit's goal has been
established is so far beyond your little conception of the
infinite that you have no idea how great the strength that
goes with you. And you can use this in perfect safety. Yet
for all its might, so great it reaches past the stars and to the

**universe that lies beyond them, your little faithlessness can
make it useless, if you would use the faithlessness instead.**
(T-17.VII.7:1-3)

What is the universe that lies beyond the stars? The usual answer
works: I don't know. Perhaps there are many universes beyond the
one we seem to "know" about.

If I picked one religion that seems most similar to ACIM it would
be non-dual Vedanta Hinduism. Sri Ramana Maharshi, who died 15
years before Jesus started giving Helen and Bill ACIM, boils it down
to this:

The world is illusion.

Brahman alone is real.

Brahman is the world.

It represents three broad stages of spirituality. First is disillusion-
ment with the world and duality. Then come the ascetic ascenders:
only God is real. Then come the hedonistic descenders: God is everything, down to the smallest grain of sand, or humble blade of grass
waiting to be eaten by a rabbit and evolve: non-duality. In terms of
course students developing a capacity to hold as true two ideas that
might seem contradictory, Ramana Maharshi's teaching is similar.
Holding Maharshi's three statements as all being true presents the
same challenge.

Let us see how this compares with the course. *The world is illusion.*
Check. *God alone is real.* Check. *God is the world.* This third statement
might not seem to agree with ACIM, maybe. Remember, the course
teaches that the problem is not the world, but a faulty perception of the
world. The world is projected; it is an external picture of an interior
state of mind. If the mind is conflicted, it will project conflict. If the
mind is healed, whole, and at peace it will project peace. Although
Jesus states emphatically that *there is no world*, He also teaches about

saving the world, with repetition. The quotes above from *The Song Of Prayer* and chapters 17 and 28 of the *Text* rather agree with part three of Ramana Maharshi's concise summary: *Forgiveness shines its merciful reprieve upon each blade of grass and feathered wing and all the living things upon the earth; the smallest leaf becomes a thing of wonder, and a blade of grass a sign of God's perfection; How holy is the smallest grain of sand, when it is recognized as being part of the completed picture of God's Son!* Here is the summary version in the course, from the *Introduction*:

> *This course can therefore be summed up very simply in this way:*
>
> **Nothing real can be threatened.**
>
> **Nothing unreal exists.**
>
> *Herein lies the peace of God.* (T-in.2:1-4)

Jesus reduces it to eight words in two short sentences. I will not claim that ACIM plagiarized Ramana Maharshi, but maybe he was part of a committee. It is possible to add one more line to Maharshi's three. If the world is illusion, and Brahman is the world, then *Brahman is illusion.* Now ACIM would never say that God is an illusion, but our *concept* of God could be. Just as we identify with an illusionary self-concept, we can believe in an illusory god-concept.

If I picked one pre-ACIM teacher who is very close to the course it would be Joel S. Goldsmith (1892-1964) who died one year before Jesus began giving the course. Thomas Merton, a mystic and hermit monk who had a lovely writing style died in 1968, during the reception of the course.

Also in the fourth chapter, I mentioned verses that brought to mind Teilhard de Chardin, who died ten years before Jesus started giving ACIM. For example: *The universe is waiting your release because it is its own.* He believed that the physical universe is evolving into a spiritual state. Is it a coincidence that one of Teilhard de Chardin's books is titled *Hymn of the Universe* (1961; English translation 1965)? *The Song Of Prayer* could be called *The Hymn of Heaven*. I am not sure it means anything, yet I find these synchronicities interesting.

Do I really need to know if Teilhard de Chardin's thought and ACIM are compatible or not? No. Do I really need to know how to integrate the two forms of metaphysics? No. I'll find out when I need to find out. There is no need to know this now. If one does not understand it, then the ideas one holds about it are nothing but speculation. Maybe this, maybe that. Maybes do not help. Jesus teaches the course with both rational and post-rational authority. The ego's thought system is pre-rational, deceptive, and insane. ACIM is not spiritual or intellectual speculation. It certainly does not mean I need to judge the value of other spiritual teachings as true or not because *There is a course for every teacher of God* (M-1.3:1), and *There are many thousands of other forms, all with the same outcome.* (M-1.4:2) In other words, the teachings of Pierre Teilhard de Chardin, or Buddha, or Rumi, or Ramana Maharshi, or Joel S. Goldsmith, or Krishnamurti, or Jesus, all have the *same outcome.* The only difference is how long they take.

> Here is the ultimate release which everyone will one day find in his own way, at his own time. You do not need this time. Time has been saved for you because you and your brother are together. This is the special means this course is using to save you time. You are not making use of the course if you insist on using means which have served others well, neglecting what was made for you. Save time for me by only this one preparation, and practice doing nothing else. "I need do nothing" is a statement of allegiance, a truly undivided loyalty. Believe it for just one instant, and you will accomplish more than is given to a century of contemplation, or of struggle against temptation. (T-18.VII.6:1-8)

The *special means* that ACIM is using to save time are the holy relationship and miracles. Previous spiritual methodologies, that arrive at the same salvation station but more slowly, are mentioned: *a century of contemplation, or of struggle against temptation.* What kind of loyalty does Jesus ask for? *Undivided.*

Ultimately, we approach the Father with *empty hands*, knowing nothing but the pure joy of gratefulness. That is an open mind. An open mind is a mind that does not judge, just as a pure heart is a heart that does not want anything but the truth of God which includes all Holiness, Knowledge, Love, Peace, and Happiness.

Remember, if you choose to join with Jesus and become a miracle-minded miracle worker, the importance of prayer, God's greatest gift to us. Miracles are maximal expressions of love. In order to extend this miraculous love, we first receive it in prayer. Remember too that the prayer Jesus teaches here is not prayer *in the usual sense.*

> *Lord, let us forgive*
>
> *Let us pray truly*
>
> *Let us heal wholly*
>
> *Let us climb the ladder of prayer as one*
>
> *Let us sing the grateful song of Union*
>
> *And Love Together forever and forever Together*

Prayer will sustain you now, and bless you as

you lift your heart to Him in rising song

that reaches higher and then higher still,

until both high and low have disappeared.

For this is prayer, and here salvation is.

This is the way. It is God's gift to you.

~ A Course In Miracles

The Foundation for Inner Peace

To learn more about *A Course In Miracles*, I encourage you to visit the website of the authorized publisher and copyright holder of the Course, the Foundation for Inner Peace: www.acim.org . While there are many excellent organizations supporting study of *A Course In Miracles*, this is the original one with the greatest variety and depth of Course-related materials, including biographies and photos of the scribes, DVDs, free access to daily Lessons, audio recordings, information about the many languages into which the Course has been translated, and electronic versions of the Course, including mobile device apps.

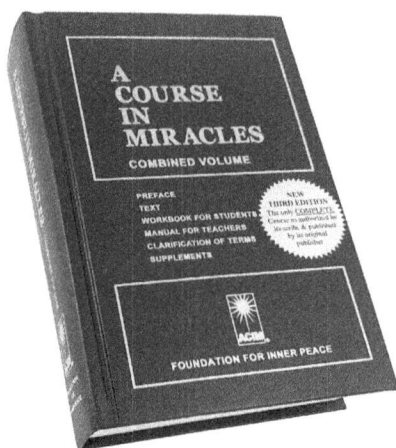

The Foundation for Inner Peace is a non-profit organization dedicated to uplifting humanity through *A Course In Miracles*. The organization depends on donations and is currently immersed in translating the Course into many languages (26 to date). The Foundation also donates thousands of copies of the Course. If you would like to support more people to benefit from *A Course In Miracles*, donating to the Foundation for Inner Peace or one of the many other fine Course-related organizations would be a worthy endeavor. A portion of the proceeds from this book will be donated to the Foundation for Inner Peace and other organizations proliferating the message of *A Course In Miracles*.

www.ingramcontent.com/pod-product-compliance
Lightning Source LLC
Chambersburg PA
CBHW020448100426
42813CB00026B/3006